Bitch
Bitch
Bitch

'BITCH! BITCH! BITCH!' is a unique collection of some of the more vindictive remarks
made around the music business in recent years. It is NOT intended to upset, offend, or add insult
to injury, but should this be the case . . . TOUGH!!!

Mike Wrenn, 1988.

Omnibus Press

London/New York/Sydney/Cologne

Bitch
Bitch
Bitch

Edited by Chris Charlesworth
Art Direction by Mike Bell
Book Designed by Giant
Picture Research by Mary McCartney
Project and typesetting co-ordinated by Caroline Watson

ISBN 0 7119 1467 2
Order No: OP44700

Exclusive distributors:

Book Sales Limited
8/9 Frith Street,
London W1V 5TZ, UK

Music Sales Corporation,
24 East 22nd Street,
New York, NY 10010, USA.

Music Sales Pty Limited,
120 Rothschild Avenue,
Rosebery, NSW 2018, Australia

To the Music Trade only
Music Sales Limited,
8/9 Frith Street,
London.W1V 5TZ, UK

Typeset by Capital Setters, London W1

Printed in England by Anchor Press, Tiptree, Essex

Picture Credits:

Arista Records
Atlantic Records
BBC
Adrian Boot
CBS
Anton Corbijn
Pati Giordano
David Koppel
LFI
Music Sales
Andy Phillips
Pictorial Press
Barry Plummer
Rough Trade
Virgin Records
Brent Walker Film Dist
David Wainwright

You know, I'm desperately trying to mention anybody else at all, because when you open a paper the first thing you home in on is some little bitchy thing or other that some star says about some other star, and it's . . . well actually, I quite like it. It's a lot more interesting than staying neutral. I remember one thing that Boy George said about George Michael that really made me crack up . . . 'He has a wonderful sense of humus.' Very droll, I thought. So anyway, I'd be grateful if you didn't mention anything I have to say about Sting. Did you know one of his first songs was called 'Don't Give Up Your Day Job' . . . I sometimes wish that boy would practise what he preached.

Paddy McAloon, Prefab Sprout, 1988.

Bachman Turner Overdrive are the only band who have a three-course meal *before* a gig.

Phil Lynott, 1978.

Prefab Sprout? . . . There's about as much sex in them as an ice-cube!

Ian McCulloch, Echo And The Bunnymen, 1984.

Mac's not what you'd call easy going. In fact he's really difficult – and arrogant. He probably sees himself as a bit of a sex symbol . . . which is a real laugh!!

Les Pattinson, Echo And The Bunnymen, on Ian McCulloch, 1985.

Don't ask me why, there's just something about standing on a stage with a guitar or a microphone that compels you to be attractive. Even Sinatra became attractive – and he's an ugly little bastard with huge flapping ears!

Robbie Coltrane, actor turned singer, 1987.

He's bloody *obese*! I mean we're talking *big* here. We're talking Moby bloody Dead Eye Dick. We're talking one of those geezers who appears in *The News Of The World* because he's *dangerously*, ticker-strainingly, *impossibly*, fat.

Steve Sutherland, journalist, on Robbie Coltrane, 1988.

Somebody should cut his tongue out.

Bobby Bluebell, on Edwyn Collins, 1984.

Cars run out of petrol trying to drive around Robbie Coltrane!

***Record Mirror* editorial, 1988.**

One thing worse than Billy Joel singing a Billy Joel song is Barry White singing a Billy Joel song. The fat prat!

Gary Bushell, journalist, reviewing 'Just The Way You Are', 1978.

What a wonderfully creative and imaginative performer Barry White is. Every song as impressive as the last. Every song the *same* as the last, in fact.

Chris Tarrant, DJ, 1988.

Boy George reminds me of an aubergine – all shiny and plump!

Paul Young, 1985.

Boy George was just a poof who hung up the coats in my club.

Rusty Egan, club owner, 1984.

I saw Boy George on *Wogan* and he spent half an hour telling everybody how clever he is. The bloke is quite sharp but he's no Bamber Gascoigne, and I can't see how anybody thinks they look good because they wear their granny's tablecloth over their head.

Pete Wylie, 1984.

I hate anything I hear by Culture Club. His voice really gets on me wick. A year ago they were all saying he's a great white soul singer – now he's just an old soddin' queen mincing around like some sickening Danny La Rue. I don't mind a *good* mincer, but he's not even that . . . Billy Idol's even worse!

Ian McCulloch, 1985.

Time Out asked me if I'm a committed drag queen or not, which pissed me off.

Committed? What's committed? How can you be committed to a pair of falsies and stilettos?

Boy George, 1984.

Gaye Advert is the only woman I know guilty of wearing more make-up than I am.

Boy George, 1983.

People say that we corrupt young kids, but there's nothing worse than kids who are gonna follow Boy George . . . For him to go out and say, 'Yeah, I'm gay and I do all these nasty things. Follow me 'cos I'm wonderful, and we'll all sing songs about being gay!' – that's really, *really* corruptible. That should be stopped. That should be wrong. Why should that cunt be allowed to go onstage and openly flaunt the fact that he's bent!?!

Abaddon, Venom, 1986.

You go to a supermarket and you see a faggot behind the fuckin' cash register, you don't want him to handle your potatoes.

Neil Young, 1985.

Lionel Richie . . . he's got a chin like an ironing board.

Pete Burns, Dead Or Alive, 1984.

Punk changed the business, but only temporarily. English pop music is still about trivia and homosexuals, isn't it?!!

Johnny Rotten, 1983.

The Pet Shop Boys are duller than the mud-caked hub-cap of a record company MD's Roller. Smoother than the chromium stair-rails in some London night-club. Cooler than a soggy Mivvi on a prickly-hot summer's day. They sound like . . . Frankie with a ball and chain.

Sandy Robertson, journalist, 1986.

I could go to a restaurant, sit down at a table and, if the waiter looked like he was really gay, I wouldn't eat my food.

Thor, 1985.

Jimmy Somerville thinks I should do more for the gay community, and he's right. I should strangle Jimmy Somerville.

Marc Almond, 1986.

This group The Sex Pistols pukes on stage? I don't necessarily like that. That's not showmanship . . . They gotta get themselves an act.

Bo Diddley, 1978.

I don't see why music has to thrive on sex and degradation. It's sick. We wouldn't have no porno freaks, or crazies with purple hair, if we all had a bit of respect.

George Benson, 1983.

How dare these young snotty-nosed kids stand up and attack established artists who have given pleasure to millions, men who know their music and have learned it the hard way. The sheer impertinence of the little brats.

Steve Harley, on punks, 1978.

Punks are the hippies of the eighties.

Gary Kemp, Spandau Ballet, 1980.

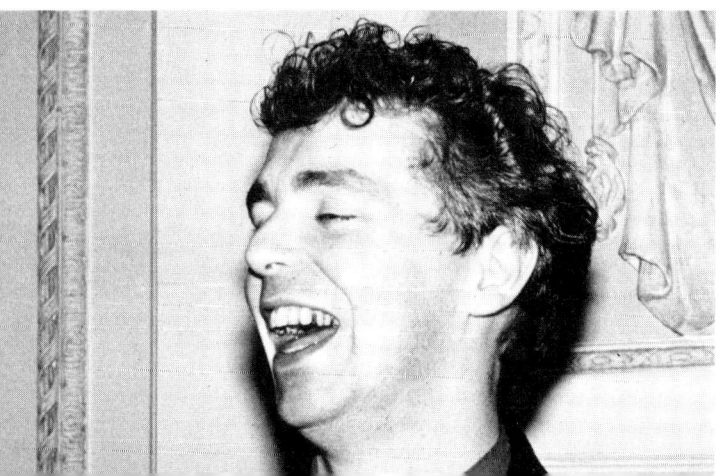

Punk rock is a bad scene, and I don't understand why it has to exist when there's so much in life.

It's terrible, a band like that being on *Top Of The Pops* – they should be on *Opportunity Knocks* if anything.

Michael Dunford, Renaissance, on Jilted John, 1978.

Why don't New Wave bands play lead breaks? – 'cause they can't!

G. Fortsch, letter to *Sounds*, 1977.

Let's get Generation X to play after The Rezillos and *before* us. Generation X are so fuckin' bad, man.

Johnny Ramone, 1978.

We were playing all this fast stuff in pubs right at the very beginning . . . before The Pistols had even started.

Knox, The Vibrators, 1983.

I don't know what they're up to, but if Adam And The Ants think they've got a tribal beat, and they use two drummers for that feeble tin-can noise which is impossible to dance to, then I'm sorry.

That's just not good enough. It might be for some, but it isn't for me.

Johnny Rotten, 1981.

In the end, I found most punks really grey and sexless. I'd rather dress up as Liberace.

Adam Ant, 1981.

He's the man who snatched defeat from the jaws of victory.

Paul Du Noyer, journalist, on Adam Ant, 1980.

Someone like Abba, or even Bucks Fizz, sound meaner to me than any of those idiot punk groups.

Nick Lowe, 1982.

The Sex Pistols were terrible live, very unprofessional, very sloppy. Johnny Rotten came over to me and said, 'What do you think?' And I said, 'I thought you guys stunk' – so he said, 'Well I think you stink too'.

Johnny Ramone, 1978.

I'm so tired of the theory of the noble savage. I'd like to hear punks who weren't at the mercy of their own rage and who could put together a coherent sentence.

Lou Reed, 1979.

The tuxedo makes him look like one of those lethal ventriloquists' dummies

that come to life and bite people's necks in old horror movies. The awkward yet artful rubber-limbed actions suggest a marionette operated by someone who's having an epileptic fit.

Giovanni Dadomo, journalist, on Johnny Rotten, 1977.

To me, the whole punk thing was totally overshadowed by what was happening down at Billy's and The Blitz. I'm sorry, but that's the way it was . . . By the end of '76, me and my mates were totally finished with punk, it was over, we wanted something new. People were coming up to me and trying to sell me Elvis Costello as a punk, you know? . . . All these geezers who had been playing in boring pub-rock bands in Dingwalls, wearing their clothes from Johnson's, and suddenly I'm supposed to regard this as punk. I just said, piss off, I'm away to find something new.

Rusty Egan, 1984.

It's reached an unthinkable state, where things are orchestrated entirely by unsympathetic and unmusical hands and ears. The people in key positions are people who don't consider pop culture to have any serious importance whatsoever.

Morrissey, 1988.

I was in a club, and a bunch of girls who didn't know who I was – but knew that I was somebody who maybe they should know – kept saying to me, 'Boy, you're really weird, what do you do?' I was rather drunk at the time, so I said the first thing that came into my head. 'Actually I used to be a male prostitute.' They said, 'Wow, what's your name?' . . . and I told them, 'Simon Le Bon'.

Marc Almond, 1982.

I love 'Tainted Love' and 'Where The Heart Is', but basically he's a pillock.

Ian McCulloch, on Marc Almond, 1984.

There really isn't any difference between Echo And The Bunnymen and Kajagoogoo. It's just that you need 'O' levels to appreciate that Echo And The Bunnymen are crap.

Pete Wylie, 1984.

I think the New Romantic thing is pathetic, they see clothes as the be-all and end-all. I'm not a wedding cake.

I've suffered for what I am, and I feel bitter about being lumped in with that lot.

Pete Burns, Dead Or Alive, 1981.

I wish I'd told a few more lies, as it gets you accepted in the right circles. I wish I had holes in me jeans, 'cos then I would have been in *The Face*.

Pete Wylie, 1983.

I like having long hair, it's no big statement. Well, I suppose it is. It means, BOG OFF *FACE* READERS.

Zodiac Mindwarp, 1986.

Zodiac won't let us talk to the press, because we'll tell them what a bastard he is.

Kid Chaos, The Love Reaction, 1987.

You've only got to read the *NME* to realise *hipness* is a pile of crap.

Ian McCulloch, 1981.

Let's face it . . . anything sounds good after punk!

Steve Harley, 1979.

The Moody Blues were everything false. From the start we were groomed into showbusiness and things got to the stage where it was all unnatural and conceived. That's why I left, actually. Nothing came from the soul, it was all contrived image – and this was the thing I wanted to get away from.

Denny Laine, 1967.

The Smiths are nonsense. Morrissey just writes negative songs about depression. Elvis Costello once said that people get the groups and music they deserve.

Pete Wylie, 1984.

I can't stand the serious young man pose. God, listen to people like Cabaret Voltaire. They sound like a Hoover with an old bag screaming over it.

Pete Burns, 1981.

There's a lot of Johnny Rotten's bastard children running the streets. They've been sold into bondage and it frightens me to see them . . . They've been sold the image of violence and they've turned it into the *reality* of violence.

Bono, U2, 1982.

My only contribution to stage invasions was to kick 'em off stage because they were getting in the way. Malcolm thought it was all wonderful. 'Look at these pictures! This'll get us publicity' – he didn't know that he was dealing with fire, because when you deal with violence the kick-backs can be so ▶

▶ strong. But I always wondered why I was the target and not him. It slightly peeves me. He's come out looking really rosy, when in fact he's just a conniving little shit. People see some sort of glamour in him being just a total bastard.

Johnny Rotten, 1978.

What I liked about Rotten was the character he played. As a guy, he was a total waste of time, a *complete* fraud.

Malcolm McLaren, 1984.

The man is a pathological liar.

Johnny Rotten, on Malcolm McLaren, 1984.

What really amuses me is the way they say that Malcolm McLaren controls the press, the media manipulator. He's done nothing. He just sat back and let them garble out their own rubbish, and they did.

Johnny Rotten 1977.

I saw him standing in snakeskin trousers with an electrified orange trumpet, playing a series of screeching notes that meant fuck all. I thought, why don't you just drive a red-hot nail through your balls.

Spike Milligan, comedian, on Miles Davis, 1988.

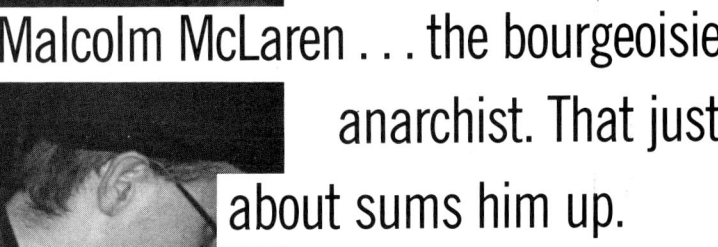

Malcolm McLaren . . . the bourgeoisie anarchist. That just about sums him up.

Johnny Rotten, 1978.

People always talk about me as a plunderer, a pirate, a plagiarist, but if they'd have said that to Picasso when he tried to imitate African art and he didn't know whether it came from Nigeria, Kenya or Timbuctoo, he would have said he didn't give a fuck. And why should he? He'd turn round and say, 'Gimme more! Plagiarism? Wonderful idea!' . . . I'd rather be a plagiarist than Nik Kershaw.

Malcolm McLaren, 1984.

It was Malcolm who made that band, when he was over here managing The Dolls. All the things he'd seen while he was over here, he projected onto The Pistols. It's always been the same though. The English take something that originated in the States – like The Stones with Chuck Berry, the whole psychedelic thing, punk . . . they refine it, then sell it back to America.

Stiv Bators, Lords Of The New Church, 1982.

I went to see Malcolm do his 'Buffalo Gals' live. It was a joke. So bad. Ludicrous. Trying to introduce that silly country and western to gangs of break-dancers . . . If ever I had to queue up to leave a venue . . .

Johnny Rotten, 1983.

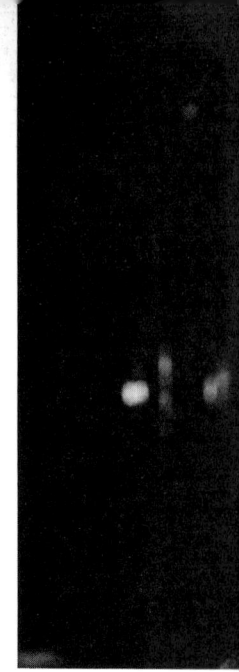

I'd say that 'Duck Rock' is the best record Trevor Horn ever made, including his Frankies and Art Of Noise. At the end of the day it's all the ideas he got off me, wonderful. And Trevor, if you hear me, good luck to you old son, you're doing a great job. Thank God you've got a bit of spontaneity, because before you met me you had none. And when I say spontaneity, I mean rock 'n' roll. Didn't have any. What was he doing? Making records with Dollar and ABC. And look at him since he made my record, look at the man . . . It's all 'Duck Rock' out-takes. All bloody ZTT is 'Duck Rock' out-takes!

Malcolm McLaren, 1984.

That record of his is like a K-Tel special.

Johnny Rotten on Malcolm McLaren, 1983.

ZTT have got a lot to answer for. They've left a trail of destruction behind them. Look how many bands they've destroyed.

Holly Johnson, on his former record label, 1988.

Trevor Horn's productions are disgusting. Trevor Horn is revolting. An ex-member of Yes and a Buggle! His style is so massively pompous and bombastic. Actually I can get really worked up about how all the old values have returned. ZTT is all production, musicianship, and hype – and people think their records are radical! Compared to something like 'God Save The Queen' being number two in Jubilee year, they're just shit!

Edwyn Collins, Orange Juice, 1984.

As far as I'm concerned, singers are people who actually live life. People talk to me about Carmel and Sade, and what do I think of the new jazz scene? *Jazz* scene?? What are you fucking talking about???

Malcolm McLaren, 1984.

I don't really think too much about her. I think she'll come and go. I'd rather stick on a Billie Holiday record, and hear the job done properly.

Johnny Marr, on Sade, 1984.

They attempt things they shouldn't attempt because they are not jazz musicians. It's all these nice little abstract notes, and it doesn't really work for me because it's not Oscar Peterson playing.

Graham Gouldman, on one-time 10cc colleagues Godley and Creme, 1978.

I don't reckon Clapton or any of your guitarists . . . I don't think you have any musicians that can really play.

Miles Davis, on the rock scene, 1971.

People were asking me then about jazz, so I used to say to these journalists, 'Who do you like? . . . Coltrane?' And they'd say, 'Who are they?'

Simon Booth, Working Week, 1984.

I met some of them and they wanted to know about Zulu Nations – do Zulu nations mean you gotta carry guns? Well, you might have to pal, but that was the South Bronx, and you live in Wood Green. I think you're gonna look ridiculous . . . but you can still bounce on your head pal, that's alright.

Malcolm McLaren, 1984.

I'll tell you, if country and western *were* the next big thing, I'd be right out there with a stetson on.

Nile Rodgers, Chic, 1979.

A lot of people in England don't *want* to think American music's any good,

despite the fact that most English music is totally ripped off.

Billy Idol, 1984.

The trouble with rock 'n' roll is that it's sex, man. Folk music is different. Take the cock out of rock and it's nothing. It's not relevant.

Don McLean, 1973.

Mick Jagger will eventually become the Chuck Berry of the sixties, constantly parodying himself on stage.

Pete Townshend, 1975.

I opened the door for a lot of people, and they just ran through and left me holding the knob.

Bo Diddley, 1971.

That boy needs his balls kicked in.

Mark E. Smith, The Fall, on spot-cream agent, Andy Kershaw.

A lot of pop TV is like *nouvelle cuisine*. It looks great, but tastes shite.

Malcolm Gerry, *Wired* producer, 1988.

That's what we call the Bo Diddley syndrome . . . where you just talk about yourself all the time. Bo Diddley used to make a lot of records all saying, basically, that he was Bo Diddley.

Kurtis Blow, 1982.

The Old Dead Squirrel Test

Popular nickname for outmoded rock show, *Old Grey Whistle Test*.

Now departed, the *Old Grey Whistle Test* represented all that was incompetent in TV rock presentation. From its hideous beginnings, where live groups like Jethro Tull would sing LP tracks, and stupid old cartoons would accompany the music of bands too embarrassed to play live, via its relatively jolly new wave Annie Nightingale years, and up to its final death throes – the sneering Hepworth, the *idiot savant* Wells, the goon Ellen and the gormless enthusiast Kershaw. The *Whistle Test* attempted to portray 'quality' and 'worth' which is interpreted as meaning groups with albums out who weren't poppy or black ... *Whistle Test* patronised us, assuming we knew nothing about an act, while *The Tube* assumed we knew nothing about anything!

David Quantick, journalist, 1988.

For years fans have been slagging off *TOTP* and *OGWT*, and calling for a new approach to rock TV. *So It Goes* was just that – and the fact that it was so much disliked says much about the innate conservatism of rock fans.

Tim Lott, journalist, 1977.

I hate my generation. I loathe and detest them with a real anger. When I did *So It Goes*, my generation turned on me with a disgust. I'd go to concerts and people would sneer at me. And at those sort of parties where people play Bob Marley all night, with a touch of The Rolling Stones, there would be an enormous hostility to me ... Now, whether kids like or dislike me in Manchester, they do remember I put The Sex Pistols on.

Tony Wilson, music biz opportunist, 1984.

The Sex Pistols ... the music may have been good, but the lyrics were more or less unlistenable. To actually sit down and listen to a Sex Pistols LP ... I mean, who'd do that? God.

Jerry Dammers, 1984.

People like The Clash always said they wouldn't do it, but ... to even be in something as corrupt as the music business is far worse than doing something stupid like *Top Of The Pops*.

Pete Wylie, 1983.

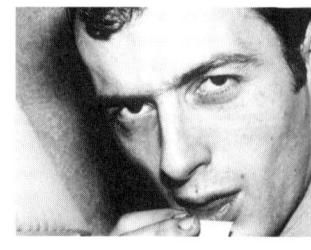

Saw a lot of the new dance bands on *Top Of The Pops* ... Why can't any of them dance?!

Ian McCulloch, 1982.

Nothing spurs you on like anger, and we were angry about all the ugly people who control this business, and all the ugly people on *Top Of The Pops*. Why all the ugliness?

Morrissey, 1983.

Looking at *Top Of The Pops* is like putting my head in the fridge in the middle of the night hoping that there's gonna be a couple of cans of beer in there, and all I can find is a couple of old, dead fish.

Tony James, Sigue Sigue Sputnik, 1985.

It's a bloody ritual. We keep sending them (*Top Of The Pops*) films of ourselves, and they keep losing them so we have to go down there and stand about like waxworks for the whole day, just to perform one lousy song.

Keith Moon, The Who, 1970.

Obviously to get on *Top Of The Pops* these days one has to be, by law, black. I think something political has happened and there has been a hefty pushing of all these black artists and all this discofied nonsense into the Top 40.

Morrissey, 1986.

The BBC, ostensibly running the ultimate non-advertising radio stations has, in Radio 1, a station that is often little more than one long commercial – a commercial for the DJs themselves, begging letters to be whisked away into the lush hinterlands of the small screen.

Julie Burchill, journalist, on *another* group of careerists.

It's society with its bow-tie under its fat chin. It always looks like it's going to go somewhere, but never does. I always look like I've been somewhere, and I have.

Roy Harper, on Radio 1, 1969.

If you view Radio 1 as being conservative, most of the commercial stations are National Front.

John Peel, DJ, 1978.

There's always one person in the audience shouting, 'Get your knickers off'– so now we're all gonna wear two pairs, and when they shout 'Get 'em off' we're gonna take one pair off and throw 'Belle Star' paper knickers into the audience.

Pennie Leyton, Belle Stars, 1981.

Even when he was young he used to get it out at discos and wave it at people.

Youth, on Zodiac Mindwarp's willy, 1986.

We called the single 'Come Back' because we hoped, with 'Come' in the title, that Mike Read would ban it.

Pete Wylie, 1984.

My mother would only object to it because it's so pathetically tepid.

John Peel, on *Your Mother Wouldn't Like It*, 1978.

Peel hates us, and we hate Peel.

Alan Horne, Postcard Records, 1981.

All in all, we think that pop stars should stick to posing for photographs, and DJs should stick to playing charity football matches.

***Melody Maker* editorial, 1983.**

Sadly, I've a few of those personal messages for you. It would be nice if we could cut down on these. It all gets rather boring, a bit like the sixties. You know, Michael has lost his insulin, that kind of thing.

John Peel, Brockwell Park CND concert, 1983.

They're always full of bikers, and their old ladies with their tits out.

Paul Weller, The Style Council, on festivals, 1985.

It was a terrible thing to do. All that crap about recording commitments. That's just the lowest bullshit I've ever

heard. They pulled out because they were scared!

Lemmy, Motorhead, on Black Sabbath's withdrawal from the Port Vale festival, 1981.

We've never done one of these festivals. What do we do if it rains? Ask everyone to start chanting for the sun to come out?

Adrian Borland, The Sound, at Glastonbury, 1981.

Look, I'm going to spend a couple of hours taking some snaps of these loonies, then I'm knobbin' off. I'd advise you to come with me . . .

Tom Sheehan, photographer, to journalistic colleague at Glastonbury, 1981.

The music's just an excuse for a scene. I personally can't listen to music in eight inches of mud, in the fairly sure knowledge that dysentery is moving around.

Robert Fripp, 1971.

A bloody mud pie job; all the hippies still lying in the mud.

Van Morrison, on Glastonbury, 1983.

Hippies with their hair cut off to make some money.

Boy George, on The Stranglers, 1983.

I think that a society that condones vaginal deodorant is a society in real trouble.

John Peel, 1985.

He's very macho, very sexist, and all those other clichés that liberal people use.

Edwyn Collins, on John Peel, 1981.

I'm not quite clear what this sexist stuff is. I think it's some cranky theory, one of those 'isms' that keep cropping up all over the place. I know that I like and respect women, and I also like fucking them. Girls *like* me, you know, and that's enough for me. If I was a creep and a sexist – or whatever you call them – if there was something wrong with me, then women wouldn't like me. The only women that *don't* like me are the ones with huge hang-ups . . . It's their problem, not mine.

Zodiac Mindwarp, 1986.

If you buy a suit in Saville Row, it costs 20 quid more to buy one for a woman, because she keeps taking it back for alterations.

Denny Laine, 1981.

The only thing girls are good for is going out shopping for glue.

Mark P, editor of *Sniffin' Glue*, 1976.

If somebody brought a man with five legs into the country, and put *him* on at Wembley, the place would be packed . . .

Jim Reid, The Jesus And Mary Chain, on Madonna's pulling power, 1987.

The shopping mall doll. Casting couches still work. For Christ's sake, she hasn't got a look and she's got dumpy body and no talent that I can see. It was either payola or the casting couch. She's gonna be a flash in the pan, hit big and disappear.

Dave Mustaine, Megadeth, on Tiffany, 1988.

The gruesome noise of corpses in the machinery.

David Stubbs, journalist, on Megadeth, 1988.

I'm parodying the male role. It seems that men have one brain in their heads and another in their penis.

Nick Gilder, 1979.

My first wife just didn't understand
what I needed.

Phil Collins, 1985

I'm afraid that I don't share most men's passion for Madonna – and I *have* seen her close-up! Neither the music nor the image inspires my loins.

David Coverdale, Whitesnake, 1988.

Madonna reinforces everything absurd and offensive. Desperate womanhood. Madonna is closer to organised prostitution than anything else.

Morrissey, 1986.

Men are all totally obsessed with their willies. That's all sex is to them. Well, that's all the *world* is to them. I mean, when those missiles go launching off Greenham Common, it won't be a 200 foot clitoris you see flying up there . . .

Jenny LeCoat, 1984.

For him to stand up there and sing about his willy for three quarters of an hour is an achievement in itself, isn't it?!

Lemmy, on Zodiac Mindwarp, 1986.

If I had a time machine I'd go back and beat up Caesar and I'd have a right go at Henry VIII. He *was* a male chauvinist wanker. I'd kick him right in the nuts.

Captain Sensible, 1981.

I've never taken 'sexism' in rock seriously, since I once spied a group of rank feminists dancing joyfully to 'Brown Sugar' at a Women's Refuge Benefit.

Steve Grant, journalist, 1986.

Sometimes a woman can really persuade you to make an asshole of yourself.

Rod Stewart, 1982.

A lot of men still look at sex as pleasing yourself – when they reach a climax, that's it!

Millie Jackson, 1985.

Pamela Stephenson's a very liberated lady and she knows her own mind. She's also got really beautiful tits.

Rowan Atkinson, comedian, 1980.

I wake up every morning with a different girl in my bed. I think I must be suffering from jet-slag.

Gary Moore, 1979.

I don't think men's bodies look good in the nude at all.

Samantha Fox, 1986.

If a 13-year-old kid puts me on their wall, it's because they're stupid!

Dr Robert, The Blow Monkeys, 1986.

I think most of them are lesbians who've got nothing better to do.

Ozzie Osbourne on the Greenham Common protestors, 1984.

Ozzy Osbourne is a moron, he couldn't carry a tune around in a suitcase.

Ronnie James Dio, Black Sabbath, 1982.

If I ever meet Ozzy, I'll bite his head off. It was disgusting what he did to that bat.

Buster Bloodvessel, Bad Manners, 1982.

There's nothing I enjoy more than being onstage and slagging off men.

Barbara Gogan, The Passions, 1980.

Barbra Streisand's a *dawg*, as is Bette Midler. I mean, she's got big tits, but thank God she's got them because she hasn't got anything else. Streisand's got long fingernails and a good voice, but her FACE! It looks as though a truck ran into it.

Divine, 1983.

He doesn't like the idea of me prissing around and being provocative in public. My father's a real drag, y'know.

Bette Midler, 1978.

Don't you stick your goddamned tongue out at me unless you intend to use it.

David Lee Roth, Van Halen, to a girl in the audience, 1984.

I don't get on with them at all, especially the ones I meet in this business. They're usually just cheap whores looking for a lay. I dislike them intensely.

Toyah, on women, 1981.

Bananarama could be any three girls. They could have been three of us – but we'd have played as well!!!

Clare, Belle Stars, 1983.

Bananarama displayed the discreet choreography of a herd of club-footed elephants . . .

***Melody Maker* review of the British Rock And Pop Awards, 1983.**

She became very uptight about things like having a laugh, and sex, and stuff like that. And she just gradually hated us more and more. She wouldn't stay on the same floor as us in the hotel, she wouldn't travel with us, she wouldn't go down in the lift with us, and she very rarely soundchecked with us. We tried. We bought her a guitar and mouth-organs and gave her credits for songs she never even wrote. We tried everything, but it *was* an uphill struggle.

Matthew Ashman, Chiefs Of Relief, on Annabella, 1984.

Women are starting to look like women again. They've got high heels and little mini-skirts and they like to go and watch a bit of cock-rock music from the hips. Bloody women in Doctor Marten's – that's what put me off rock 'n' roll for a while.

Gary Holton, 1984.

There are so many loose women around, and I find that appalling. Our lyrics tend to reflect this attitude, so normally they're appalling too!

Lips, Anvil, 1983.

To become a member of Women's Lib you have to have no tits.

Ian McNab, Icicle Works, 1986.

. . . On the flip side you'll find live covers of 'Should I Stay Or Should I Go' and 'Roadhouse Blues' – probably a clearer indication of where their heads are at just now. Up their arses if you ask me.

Helen Fitzgerald, journalist, reviewing 'Who Do You Want For Your Love' by The Icicle Works, 1986.

Reggae is to me the most racist music in the world. It's an absolute total glorification of black supremacy.

Morrissey, 1986.

Once upon a time it was enough to know that U2 are crap. But not any more. Now you've got to know *why* they're crap.

Julian Cope, 1983.

All the so-called liberators spout excessive hatred. On the one side, feminists scream men are the enemies . . . on the other extreme it's the Tetley Bittermen thing. I refuse to recognise the terms hetero-, bi-, and homo-sexual. Everybody has exactly the same sexual needs. People are just – sexual, the prefix is immaterial.

Morrissey, 1984.

The world dictates that heteros make love, while gays have sex.

Boy George, 1984.

Whenever my girlfriend wears tights, I refuse to see her. I put her on the first train back to Hornchurch and tell her to come back wearing suspenders.

William Reid, The Jesus And Mary Chain, 1985.

Sexism is just an extension of racism.

Zaf, Rock Against Racism, 1981.

Ray Charles is nothing but a blind ignorant nigger.

Elvis Costello, 1979.

Bollocks!

Ade Edmondson, comedian, 1985.

I read in this French magazine, Jim Kerr saying that I say all these things about them because I'm insecure. That's ridiculous. He regarded us as the black sheep of the family – the family being us, U2, Simple Minds and Big Country. I thought that was telling. In order for that family to mean anything, it 'as to have us in it. We give them credibility. We've just been lumped in with 'em through no fault of our own. The others are all in the same colostomy bag. And as for Bono, 'e needs a colostomy bag for his mouth!

Ian McCulloch, 1984.

Bono's taken it into his head that he knows what's good for everyone, and I can't do that . . . We're not an anthem band. I look at U2 lyrics and they don't make any sense, they're just sentences disassociated from each other, put into places where the music makes them sound good.

Mick Lynch, Stump, 1988.

Who buys U2 records anyway? It's just music for plumbers and bricklayers. Bono, worra slob. Yer'd think with all that climbin' about he does he'd look real fit an' that. But he's real fat, yer know. Reminds me of a soddin' mountain goat.

Ian McCulloch, 1984.

Glenn Phillips: a rumour in his own time.

Sounds picture caption, 1977.

I didn't even feel sorry for him when he died.

Lou Reed, on Jim Morrison, 1977.

Apartheid was exported to the rest of the world from Queensland.

Bart Willoughby, of Australian aboriginal group, No Fixed Address, 1984.

When I toured with The Stones, the audience would come up to me after the show and say, 'Man, you're really good, you ought to record' – how do you think that makes me feel after 25 years in the business?

Bobby Womack, 1984.

Being non-sexist, non-racist etc has become so phoney – it's well out of hand. I don't think there's anything wrong in being prejudiced – it's only wrong against someone who's got enough problems already. Like, I don't mind being prejudiced against the Japanese.

Alexei Sayle, comedian, 1984.

COUNTDOWN TO LETHARGY

Headline to Steve Miller feature, NME, 1975.

I think Diana Ross is awful.

Morrissey, 1986.

Diana Ross is great as a *person* – she hasn't had a good *record* in her time.

Lou Reed, from his 'Take No Prisoners' LP, 1978.

In assessing Lou Reed's 'Metal Machine Music' some important considerations should be borne in mind . . . the music inside is largely irrelevant.

Ed Ward, journalist, 1975.

I wouldn't have thought any band could make it with a W.C. Fields lookalike for a singer. If Jim Morrison had looked like Jim Kerr, he'd still be alive.

Ian McCulloch, on Simple Minds, 1984.

Sounds? I always associate *Sounds* with colour posters of Brian Connolly of Sweet.

Ian McCulloch, 1984.

The transformation of precious jewels and gold into lead.

Charles Shaar Murray, journalist, defining heavy metal, 1984.

Not only did every guitarist learn to speak the new language, but they all began to repeat the same sentence . . . an unforgivable grim cavalcade of mindless and hysterical riffs, perpetuated by the kind of people who saw nothing more challenging in the instrument than a socially acceptable means of pointing their willies at an audience.

Bill Nelson, on the rise of heavy metal, 1984.

Purple was a complete ego-maniac band.

Ian Paice, 1983.

I never really heard Geezer (Butler) make any decision, other than to have another pint.

Ronnie James Dio, 1983.

April Wine sounds more like the title of a Barbara Cartland novel than the name of a rock band. Quite appropriate, as April Wine are to heavy metal, as Cartland is to Tolstoy. I'm not saying their album is lightweight, but I had to staple it to my desk to stop it floating out of the window.

Heavy Metal Heather, journalist and publicist, 1984.

If I had a rotating keyboard stand, then Carl Palmer would *insist* on having a revolving drum riser – and Greg Lake *had* to have something as well . . .

Keith Emerson, 1983.

We ended up on the floor like two tarts having a scrap. Now he's a marked man. If I ever meet Ritchie Blackmore again there will be trouble.

David Coverdale, on his one-time Deep Purple colleague, 1981.

I never get aggro. I'm pretty butch. Like the guy came up to me at the airport and said, 'My chick fancies you'. So I say, 'Well cool, I'm probably a better lay than you are'.

Marc Bolan, 1972.

Bolan knows that he didn't have a hit until we sang on his records.

Mark Volman and Howard Kaylan, 1972.

Donny (Osmond) is a right Charlie, Jimmy (Osmond) makes me puke . . . Bolan's had his day.

Judge Dread, 1973.

Bolan isn't camp – he's prissy, and fey, and engrossed in his own image.

David Bowie, 1972.

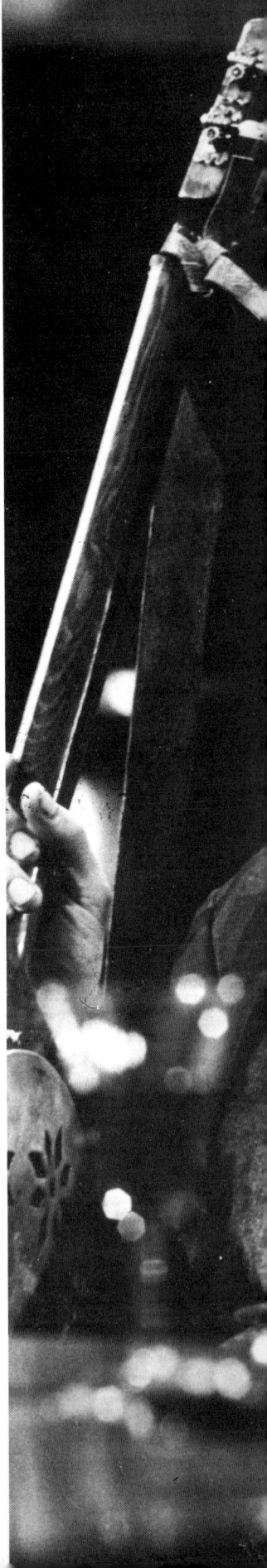

David Bowie is a very good friend of mine . . . A lot of people think he gave me all his old dresses.

Boy George, 1983.

I went to see David Bowie. I don't like to be left out. He arrived in this giant glass spider and I thought, does it make the song any better? Why not do it with exploding boots? Or in a fish tank???

Spike Milligan, 1988.

The new romantics owed everything to Bowie. He did it more, he did it better, and he did it before. And it got to the point with the 'Ziggy Stardust' stuff where it frightened him because he was getting a result that makes anything that's happened since pale. And he backed off because he didn't want to deal with the amount of control he had . . . What a wimp!!

Jerry Casale, Devo, 1981.

David Bowie is not an actor. Someone like Bowie just seems to worry whether the make-up's right, and whether the camera's on his good side.

Johnny Rotten, 1983.

My son likes Madness. I thought he was going to start liking Flock Of Seagulls, which worried me a lot, ha-ha!

David Bowie, 1983.

Ahmet auditioned for a television series yesterday, to play a character named Stinky in a showtime sitcom. He's 12-years-old and he's not afraid to say anything to anybody. He was reading in this room for the producers, and there were these howls of laughter. Ahmet came out, and my wife asked what happened. 'Well' he said, 'They liked me. They said they were going to bring me back to read again. I told them, 'I hope to God it's not written by the guy who wrote this crap.' Ha-ha!

Frank Zappa, on his son, 1985.

I enjoyed those shows I did in London at The Rainbow . . . I kept thinking, Frank Zappa fell 17 feet down into that pit. I hate Frank Zappa, and it made me so happy to think about that.

Lou Reed, 1975.

We got rid of our drummer after our first gig owing to musical differences. We were musical, he was different.

Dave Holmes, Dr Filth, 1982.

The Damned are a very dirty version of The Bay City Rollers . . . or Eddie And The Hot Rods with make-up.

Johnny Rotten, 1977.

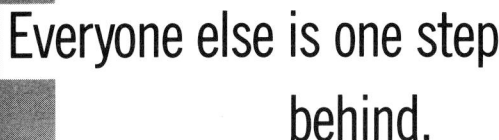

Everyone else is one step behind.

David Bowie, 1982.

I lost all my friends in the Bay City Rollers disaster of '74. It was like some plague, a complete wipe-out. They never had one good song. They couldn't scrape up one attractive feature between them. Yet girls went ape for them. I see echoes in the lure of Manilow, and I think there must be some theory to it – the call of the mild perhaps.

Julie Burchill, journalist, 1984.

Julie Burchill just makes me really sick, you know. She's just the Glenda Slag of modern pop writing.

Elvis Costello, 1983.

I don't think Elvis Costello is too much of a lyricist. People call him a great poet – I think they're off their rocker.

Steve Wynn, Dream Syndicate, 1984.

A lot of writers tell me about soul and know nothing about it – they've probably got 'Al Green's Greatest Hits' and they think they can write the book of soul. People like Paolo Hewitt – I reckon he knows fuck all about it.

Mick Hucknall, Simply Red, 1986.

I'm not interested in blues or soul music . . . I haven't been in many cottonfields recently, know what I mean?

Tony James, 1985.

Johnny Rotten is all mouth and trousers, the sort of hypocrite who believes it is his divine right to have one law for himself and one law for everybody else. John's the perfect Reggie Kray type, getting others to do his violence for him while he just mouths-off.

Glen Matlock, The Sex Pistols, 1978.

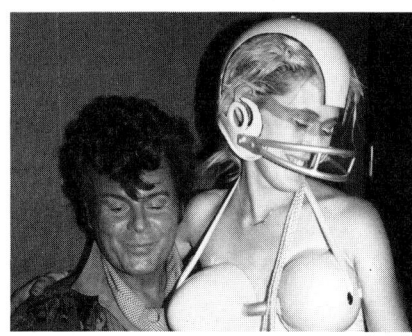

Gary Glitter's show was frankly banal, vulgar and slightly fake in the highest traditions of rock 'n' roll. It was fabulous!

Alan Clayson, letter to the *Melody Maker*, 1981.

DEVO – THE FIVE VEGETABLES OF THE APOCALYPSE.

NME headline, 1978.

To me, Barry Manilow is insane and emotionally bankrupt. His ideas of love and emotions are the same as soap operas and *Love Boat*, which I think are totally foul.

Mark Mothersbaugh, Devo, 1983.

If I wore a kilt, played a synthesiser and came up with a lot of old waffle that passed itself off as profound, I'd probably make it.

Lee Fardon, 1981.

The *NME* has become like a cross between the *Financial Times* and the *Whole Earth Catalogue*.

Lemmy, Motorhead, 1984.

Do you remember when you were at school and you used to have a satchel? Remember how great it was to write the names of your favourite bands all over it? Didn't it feel great if you wrote down the name of a group that no-one else had heard of, even better if later they had a hit record, all the kids thinking 'Hey, he was going on about them ages ago'? I can laugh at it now, but it was a sad day when I finally threw away my satchel. When are your writers going to throw away theirs?

Steve, Worcester, letter to the NME, 1980.

I just get speechless with rage about the press . . . I have to control myself from going round and sorting some of them out.

Joe Strummer, The Clash, 1978.

Every journalist and his brother has a horror-story concerning John Lydon (alias Rotten). Especially the ones who've never met him.

Andy Strickland, journalist, 1986.

You still workin' for the *Melody Maker*, trying to influence the diseased minds of the cretins?

Lou Reed, greeting Allan Jones, journalist, 1978.

I don't talk to that many people. I do most of the talking because I deserve to. If somebody's faster and smarter than me, I'd shut up and listen . . . It doesn't happen too often, though.

Lou Reed, 1978.

I wish we had their ticket sales – we could buy a new box of matches.

Pete, Motorhead, on Sigue Sigue Sputnik, 1986.

The critics tried to kill this band and, in not succeeding, it just shows how powerless they are.

Andy Taylor, on his days with Duran Duran, 1983.

Since 1975 the rock press have hated disco and anything to do with funk. Probably because it was too honest-to-goodness working class for them.

Gary Kemp, Spandau Ballet, 1981.

An artist composes for himself and the public, not for critics. I don't have much confidence in critics, but myself and the public don't get a chance of reviewing my albums.

Al Kooper, 1971.

I read that bloody review and it's all about this guy who supposedly spent £395 a night on a hotel room, and consequently has nothing to say to humanity. To think that *Melody Maker* has somebody like that writing for them . . . to think they have somebody with insufficient brains, who believes I'm dumb enough to pay £395 for a hotel room! He doesn't deserve to write the ads at the bloody back.

Bryan Ferry, on Chris Brazier, 1978.

In a lot of cases, critics have been taking advantage of their unassailable position to be abusive.

Terry Ellis, manager of Jethro Tull, 1973.

Listening to Rush is as mesmeric an experience as watching someone hand emboss flock wallpaper.

The Stud Brothers, journalist(s), 1988.

What the hell are you . . . an arsehole or something? Is that what you're trying to ►

I just heard on the radio a very deep Kevin 'no press interviews' Rowland of Dexy's. I'd say he needs all the misquoting he can get.

Alan Charles, Leamington, letter to the *NME*, 1980.

▶ say? I'm reasonable, I don't mind saying it. You've probably noticed over the past few minutes, I haven't reacted. I haven't *slugged* you.

Kirk Brandon, Spear Of Destiny, exchanging pleasantries with an *NME* journalist, 1984.

Oh gawd! Having spent two weeks soaking up the latest Spear Of Destiny album prior to meeting young Kirkypoos, the last thing I needed was to open up the *NME* three hours before our collision and find that in 'The Night Of The Long Nose' some wilting dufflecoat had decided to dump his rusty nuts on our hero. I was apparently on my way to meet an insane, one-legged Austrian neo-fascist, controlling plentiful shares in Rio Tinto Zinc, a vast alternative fan club in Argentina and a curiously mobile monocle. And you can't say fuhrer than that.

Mick Mercer, journalist, 1984.

An ex-member of Theatre Of Hate gave me the advice (about Kirk Brandon). 'Just sit back, take in all his bullshit – then go away and slag him off!' . . .

Johnny Waller, journalist, 1983.

Kirk actually says something to young kids who are growing up, who *are* the future. We hope those young kids will like what he's said, and work it out for themselves. And we don't need stupid journalists to explain that to anyone.

Terry Razor, manager of Kirk Brandon, 1983.

The trouble with most of the writers around at the moment, is that they can't write, which is quite a big drawback.

Clive James, writer and critic, 1973.

It is very satisfying to know that my audience continues to attend my concerts in spite of the fact that cynical rags like *Melody Maker* continue to sell the disco junk and glitter trash and make the commercial music scene the perverted cesspool it has become, awash with no-talent clowns who do anything to sell records, except make decent music.

Don McLean, 1978.

Don't give up your paper rounds, lads, leave it to the experts.

John Cooper-Clarke, on Seething Wells, Attila The Stockbroker et al, 1982.

Melody Maker is an indispensable music paper. I always check it out to discover if I've retired again.

Leonard Cohen, 1976.

Look, I'm sick of this interview! Why won't you say anything? I ask you perfectly answerable questions and you just say 'yes' or 'no'.

Rose Rouse, journalist, in 'conversation' with Jean Jacques Burnel, The Stranglers, 1982.

Is it true you can't gerra job on the *Melody Maker* these days if you don't like Elvis Costello?

Ian McCulloch, 1984.

I don't read the music papers much, y'know. They're full of people that think they're literary geniuses, putting things in brackets 'cos they've just read a bit of Thomas Pynchon.

Graham Parker, 1982.

Listen man, don't you realise that 90 per cent of the people in this world are fuckin' sheep? No? Well, then you're one of them. And you better believe it, motherfucker! Baaaaaaa! Hey, just get outa here, okay?! There's three more bimboes I got to see, I can't waste my time.

Willy De Ville, passing the time of day with the *NME*, 1978.

My worst experience in pop? Being interviewed by Robin Smith.

Tracie Young, on a *Record Mirror* hack, 1983.

We think that 80 per cent of the people who write in the papers ought to be shot.

Jeff Blythe, The Bureau, 1981.

Y'know, if I turned in some of that stuff when I was in the seventh grade, they would have kicked my ass!

Gil Scott Heron, on music journalism, 1982.

The music papers have a very set idea of the social system. Punk conveniently fitted their archetypal view of working class street credibility. We threaten the established pattern and they just can't stand it.

Gary Kemp, 1981.

You don't get into *Smash Hits* unless you're very lucky or you've got a Top 40 hit. It's like, if it isn't a commercial success, it can't be any good, but that's just not true.

Jerry Dammers, 1983.

It's like the manager of Rotherham United saying Liverpool are shit.

Ian McCulloch, on Biba Kopf's review of 'Ocean Rain', 1984.

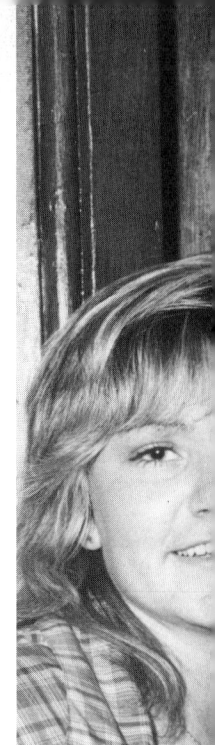

I don't care if *Record Mirror*, *Smash Hits* or *No.1* ever print anything about us again. As far as I'm concerned they deal in complete shit.

Stuart Adamson, Big Country, 1983.

Journalists? . . . I make a point of sleeping with the people who interview me. It's the only way to the top. I just wish they were better in bed.

Momus, 1988.

Did you hear about the *Smash Hits* 'journalist' who was such a cretin the others noticed.

Anonymous graffiti, Carnaby Street, London.

Spandau Ballet! . . . Amateur hour!! Stuff like jamming at rehearsals which you'd chuck out and wouldn't consider putting on plastic. To them, that's a *tour de force*.

Johnny Rotten, 1981.

They may have passion in their blood, but there's lead in their boots.

Paul Colbert, journalist, on Tandoori Cassette, 1983.

I've been sat here knowing this was in the pile but afraid to touch it.

Billy Mann, journalist, reviewing Spandau Ballet's 'Fight For Ourselves' single, 1986.

You can't drink on an eight-hour flight, pass out, and then go on stage . . . Well, you can, but then you're Spandau Ballet.

Robert Smith, The Cure, 1985.

I saw that poster announcing the return of Spandau Ballet, and I just thought, 'God forbid!' Urrgh!!

Peter Hook, New Order, 1986.

There are too many microwave bands around. They look good on the surface, but as soon as you stick your knife in . . .

Martin Fry, ABC, 1982.

Rick Astley thought we were the worst band he'd ever heard . . . that's a great compliment. We were really proud of it.

Kev Hopper, Stump, 1988.

In times of the wildest optimism or the deepest pessimism we have heroes who disturb us, who are outrageous and flamboyant, who offer unsettling critiques of the way we live, who expose our deepest psychic secrets or use their music to mount an attack on all we hold most dear, encapsulating in a

single intoxicating burst the restless aspiration of a generation. In 1988 we have Rick Astley.

Momus, 1988.

We love Rick Astley, we love Duran, We love Stock Aitken and Waterman, But when it comes to The Mission – yuck!

Funk Rhythm Dadda, *Melody Maker* letters, 1988.

Wayne. The name Wayne. Think of all the Waynes you know. Do any of those Waynes distinguish themselves from any of the Darryls, Darrens, Dannys or Garys that you know? If we were to say to you, 'We've got this friend you've *got* to meet, his name's Wayne' – would you think 'Ah good, here's a bloke who in sorrow is driven by habits of serious reflection, a geezer from whose grief-stricken heart has wrung the finest wine, a chap, nay a nightingale, who sits in darkness and sings to cheer his own solitude with the sweet sound of melancholy, a guy who'll never mistake

Echo And The Bunnymen for metaphysics?' No. When you hear the name Wayne, you think WALLY, you think HAIRY DASHBOARD, you think PRIOR ENGAGEMENT.

The Stud Brothers, journalist(s), on Wayne Hussey of The Mission, 1988.

In 10 years time All About Eve will be living in California, and taking five years to make a record.

Penny Kiley, journalist, 1988.

Black Lace? What's that??

Russ Abbot, comedian, 1985.

If I go round to someone's house and there's an Eric Clapton record in their collection, I just walk out.

Jon Moss, Culture Club, 1985.

We have far greater power over our audience than Paul Weller will ever have with his, because we really could stand on stage and say, 'Go out and break the walls of Babylon NOW!' . . . and they would.

John Taylor, Duran Duran, 1982.

A face like a bucket with a dent in it!

**Allan Jones, journalist, on
Feargal Sharkey, 1988.**

What is it about the hapless Feargal
Sharkey that inflames my imagination
with dreams of homicide, the nailing of
his head to any available surface?
Could it be his, well, *distinctive* looks,
features whose inverse superstructure
many find uniquely unsettling? Perhaps
it's Feargal's voice, that dreadful
whistle whose contracted tones sound
like they may be better employed as the
emergency signature that calls
lifeboatmen to sea in stormy weather?
More probably it's the songs that he has
the audacity to record, which are
invariably so offensively trite that one
wishes they had remained forever in
their cage, fed on scraps . . .

Allan Jones, journalist, 1988.

Let's name names – Wham!, Spandau,
The Thompson Twins, Howard Jones,
Frankie, Duran Duran etc, etc . . . the

positive proof that capitalism does not
work. The sons and daughters of
Thatcherism and the new Right. They
want to be dipped in honey, and rolled
in clover. Now – wouldn't it be kinder to
pour on petrol and get rid of the lot?!

Paul Weller, 1985.

It's way out of proportion that my
haircut got front page next to 30,000
people dying in an Indian disaster. It
makes me quite sick.

**Simon Le Bon, Duran Duran,
1985.**

You can learn how *not* to treat people.

**Gary Simpson, Le Mat, when
asked whether there was
anything to be learnt from Duran
Duran, 1983.**

Duran Duran are completely disgusting,
and crass, and offensive.

Mick Hucknall, Simply Red, 1985.

Simon Le Bon's got a fucking huge nose.

Tracie Young, 1985.

If we were all devastatingly handsome
and actually liked one another, we'd
probably be Duran Duran or the biggest
band on earth. As it is, I'm actually
quite a decent chap, and the rest of the
group are wankers.

**Jools Holland, on his role with
Squeeze, 1985.**

Sigue Sigue Sputnik are a joke. They're like something out of Boots the chemists.

Johnny Rotten, 1986.

Stop knocking Sputnik – it's not their fault they're midgets.

Andy Gill, journalist, 1986.

I'll say something for Duran Duran, they have really nice hair. They can't play their instruments, they write really crappy songs and their music sucks. But when it comes to hair, they've got it!

Ad-Rock, The Beastie Boys, 1987.

Culture Club are obnoxious. They're just geared towards being number one.

Ian McCulloch, Echo And The Bunnymen, 1984.

I read people saying that 'Karma Chameleon' was a brilliant record, and I think anybody who says that needs their head reading.

Pete Burns, Dead Or Alive, 1984.

I got a message from Boy George, through Peter Powell, saying let's be friends. I said fuck off, I don't speak to men in dresses.

Pete Burns, Dead Or Alive, 1984.

A bit of National Service would do him good. He's a fat sod.

Ian McCulloch, on Boy George, 1984.

Wham! are really good and he's got a good voice, but please, the hair, the *hair* . . .

Boy George, 1984.

What annoys me is that *he* gets to wiggle his bum, and no-one slags *him* off. What's so credible about his buttocks compared to mine?

George Michael, on Bruce Springsteen, 1985.

I heard George Michael's 'I Want Your Sex' quite recently in the car. I wasn't deeply impressed. I thought it sounded like Ponce, I mean Prince.

Morrissey, 1985.

I don't like the crappy slogans they've got. 'Make It Big' and 'Go For It'. Go for fucking what? What exactly are they going for? An all year suntan??

Paul Weller, on Wham!, 1985.

Janet Jackson, Whitney Houston. I hate all those records in the Top 40 – I think they're vile in the extreme.

Morrissey, 1986.

I still detest the people in the Top 10 as much as I did when we started.
Robert Smith, The Cure, 1985.

If something was in the charts, I wouldn't buy it. I couldn't have pop stars in my record collection!
Nik Kershaw, 1984.

I like Chuck Berry and Howlin' Wolf and Robert Johnson, and I like Hoagy Carmichael – those things are great and they'll always be great. I can't say the same about fuckin' Nik Kershaw – I don't think that's ever gonna be great, I don't even think it's great now.
Mick Jones, B.A.D., 1986.

The majority of pop stars are complete idiots in every respect.
Sade, 1985.

Most pop music is revivalist nonsense.
Tony James, 1985.

Gary Kemp: I'm looking forward to Canada . . . I mean it's, like, *Love Story* country.
Nick Heyward: It was made in Boston, ya wally.
1984.

When record companies pump all their money into bands like Eighth Wonder,

they obviously don't know what they're doing.
Frank, June Brides, 1985.

With all due respect to Prince, it's hard to think of anybody stepping out of the way as he was coming, y'know what I mean?
Walter Hill, director, 1984.

The Jesus And Mary Chain deserve a good clip around the ear. They're a load of cack.
Rat Scabies, The Damned, 1985.

The Thompson Twins, Howard Jones and Nik Kershaw are the epitome of what is wrong with either the music industry, or the record buying public. Everybody has got so used to safe, tidy music and unimaginative lyrics.
Johnny Marr, The Smiths, 1984.

My favourite Thompson Twins single? . . . Is it possible to have one? Well, if I'm horribly tortured and flogged to admit it . . . I think I'd rather face further flogging.
Morrissey, 1984.

Compulsive, low-profile disco insinuations from the singular Mr Stewart. Do we detect the creeping,

side-winding groove of Simon Climie at work? WE DO! Oh, bugger.

Myrna Minkoff, journalist, reviewing Jermaine Stewart's 'Get Lucky', 1988.

Up until The Style Council I maintained, and I still maintain, that pop music is for wallies.

Steve White, The Style Council, 1985.

More Johnny's Curiosity Killed The Wet Bros.

Tony Reed, journalist, on Habit, 1988.

Not worth talking about. All that wimpy stuff is no threat to anybody . . . Did you see that spotty Ben Perrier Water bloke on *Network 7*. They asked him, 'When did you first masturbate?' Ha-ha-ha! He went so red. I thought he was going to ask, 'Why, does it show?' Ha-ha-ha!!

Johnny Rotten, on Curiosity Killed The Cat, 1987.

Pretty boy pop is for budgerigars.

Sue Lawley, TV presenter, 1983.

I don't need to open sports shops in Edgware to get number ones.

Dave Stewart, Eurythmics, 1981.

Who will deliver us from Ben Elton? . . . As Joe Strummer so candidly remarked t'other night, Elton's self-righteousness is now approaching dizzying heights of sanctimonious self-regard, and what previously was honourably right-on is now a bit of a write-off. The old motormouth delivery has also accelerated to the point where Elton's in grave danger of turning into the David Coleman of alternative comedy, with punch-lines garbled and entire stretches of monologue rendered well-nigh unlistenable by the performer's ranting hysteria.

Allan Jones, journalist, 1988.

Television still has this mystical ability to separate you from the world and confer importance upon you. I've never understood that. I can't understand people who find it a great joy to send off

to Simon Bates and get him to mention their Uncle Bert on the air.

Morrissey, 1984.

It's like going to the launderette. You dread it, don't want to do it, then it's just over so quick. *And* you get £50 each.

Henry Priestman, The Christians, on doing children's TV, 1988.

It's completely and entirely impossible to care for the characters in *Crossroads*. David Hunter was in the programme for 50 years, and I still wouldn't recognise him if he was dancing on that table now.

Morrissey, 1985.

Selina Scott is awful on *The Clothes Show*, embarrassing when she stands in for *Wogan*, but her worst hour was the show when she went round the country interviewing people and asking monks about their sex life. Let's start a campaign to rid this country of this appalling woman, and then work towards abolishing the other ditsys.

Magenta Devine, TV presenter and pop publicist, 1988.

Every time they break into a song, the legs fly apart, the old arms start flapping up and down, and the mouth

gapes open. They manage to look like nothing more than patients with a toothache who like a little tune or two.

Suzi Quatro, on TV serial *Rock Follies*, 1977.

Does this mean I don't have to do *The Merv Griffin Show*!?!

Peter Frampton, following his near fatal car crash, 1978.

David Attenborough, when he does these documentaries, he doesn't understand a thing. 'Hello viewers, here's a native eating a berry.' And there's this guy chewing on a hallucinogenic staring at the camera like he's on another planet. And David Attenborough's there telling you why he's wearing a colourful head-dress. I'll tell you why. 'Cos it looks fuckin' great. You're out of your fuckin' head, and you're dancing around all painted up. There aren't any sociological reasons – they're just having a good time. And that's what we're doing.

Zodiac Mindwarp, 1986.

Terry Wogan uses his guests as a springboard for what he wants to say next. He might as well have a bowl of mashed potatoes on.

Annie Anxiety, 1988.

The telly here is appalling. It's disgraceful, no imagination at all.

EastEnders is the worst thing I've seen in my life.

Johnny Rotten, 1986.

When someone like Princess Diana turns round and says 'Don't take smack' – that makes me want to take it.

Rat Scabies, The Damned, 1985.

Okay, I admit I'm a bit of a speed freak, but I never touch smack. Besides, people who like smack also like Lou Reed, and that can't be anything in its favour.

Lemmy, Motorhead, 1979.

For a nation that can put a man on the moon, it isn't that much of a problem to find a cure for heroin addiction – not if they *really* wanted to.

Keith Richards, 1972.

I don't see the point in the anti-heroin campaign. There are more serious problems in the world than some stupid bastards who get themselves addicted to heroin.

William Reid, The Jesus And Mary Chain, 1985.

I can understand why people up in tower blocks in Manchester or Liverpool, or somewhere are doing drugs. That escapism, and kind of immediate good ▶

feeling must be something when you're leading such an awful life. What *does* annoy me, is all these poor little rich kids, taking drugs just for something to do. They're born with a silver syringe in their mouths. As far as I'm concerned, let them fucking die.

Matt Johnson, The The, 1986.

The machine had a better sense of humour, and it didn't smoke so much dope either.

Ian McCulloch, Echo And The Bunnymen, on drummer Pete de Freitas' arrival in the ranks, 1983.

As I watch the world drift by from my eyrie at *Melody Maker*, I can see two pigeons trying to get their wings over on a narrow ledge halfway up the opposite building. The male pigeon hobbles after the female until it reaches the end of the precipice and teeters on the brink of a nuptial downfall in High Holborn. At this point the female takes off, glides in a short arc to land behind the male, then staggers away in the opposite direction. The geezer pigeon, on the other hand, spends a heart-stopping few moments spinning round on one leg before toeing it after his girlfriend at maximum revs only to catch up with her at the far end, where the entire process is repeated. There must be a reason for this, in the same way that there must be a reason for Bauhaus, though I'm damned if I can find it.

Paul Colbert, journalist, 1983.

The Bunnymen were psychedelic, but God they nearly broke their bollocks trying to be. Walking around pretending they were on acid . . .

Pete Burns, Dead Or Alive, 1983.

Whoever the turd was who first said that, they should chop his head off! It only takes one person to say it. Somebody could say we were wall to wall music, and everyone else would start saying that. Nobody knows what it meant. It doesn't mean anything, *psychedelic*. Now, if rock critics could learn to be as original as we are . . .

Ian McCulloch, 1981.

It revolves round that studied look of the packet of Woodbines in the pocket – who the sod smokes Woodbines? Can't even

find them. Must take them longer finding a place that sells the right cigarettes, than writing a good song!!

Ian McCulloch, on The Redskins' image, 1984.

Have you ever seen a photo of The Redskins where Chris Dean *isn't* snarling? I've never seen such snarling.

Chris Maund, Mighty Ballistics Hi-Power, 1986.

They may call me an uncaring sexist fascist, but I care about people much more than monsters like The Redskins do. Hatred is their message. 'What's the point in winning if we don't shoot the bastards.' That was in one of their songs! I mean fuckin' 'ell, that was played on Radio 1 yet they won't play my songs about making love to women.

Zodiac Mindwarp, 1986.

When I got battered in York by a bouncer, I was trying to protect the audience from being battered. That was the whole reason why I got done in after the gig. A bouncer was beating on a kid in the front, and I tried to get him with me mikestand – and he battered me afterwards. And me wife was there, and she heard the Redskins say, really glad, serves him right. And they're the voice of youth! I don't know what they'd have

done. Those kind of people'd write a song about the kid being battered rather than *do* anything about it.

Ian McCulloch, 1984.

Fox-hunting is like a lot of establishment things – just because people have been doing it for hundreds and hundreds of years, it's supposed to make it okay. But it doesn't. There's nothing you can say to these people. You can't raise any reasonable arguments with people like that . . . I suppose the only way to deal with them is to get rid of them. I don't know what else you can do but shoot them.

Paul Weller, 1975.

We're in a political party and Weller's not.

X Moore, The Redskins, 1984.

Paul Weller? . . . He's the biggest divvy of them all. Saw him on the telly with that Mick Talbot, y'know, one of the greatest geniuses of our time. It was from Paris or somewhere an' they were talking about 'Cafe Bleu' or something . . . Ha! . . . He's probably bought a packet of Gitanes once in his life and he doesn't like the taste, but the packet looks better than a packet of Rothmans . . . Street credibility? He wouldn't know ▶

▶ a paving stone if it hit 'im on the head!
... He's just a skinny twat who 'as the
worst haircut going. Totally asexual!

Ian McCulloch, 1984.

The Alarm are the sort of band who will
sing endlessly about revolution or
storming the Winter Palace or whatever
... and they probably never stood on a
picket line or leafleted a rent strike.

X Moore, 1984.

Anyone in their late-twenties who
dresses up like a skinhead is a fucking
retard as far as I'm concerned.

**Mark E. Smith, on The Redskins,
1986.**

Paul Weller? ... He was a Tory five years
ago, but now he's like Ken Livingstone's
mannequin. I just think he's as thick as
two short planks ... a non-entity. There
was a headline in one of the music
papers the other day – 'Paul Weller
Angry At Death Of Taxi Driver'– or
something. Who *cares* if Paul Weller's

angry about it? Obviously it was a bad
thing to happen, but you don't have to
issue statements saying how angry you
are. People who are attracted by that
are just little soddin' deadbeats who
need someone like him to give them an
excuse for being the scum of the earth.
People are so soddin' thick.

Ian McCulloch, 1985.

Walk down a street, stop 10 people, and
I'll bet nine of them will be complete
pricks.

**Jim Reid, The Jesus And Mary
Chain, 1985.**

Paul Weller knocks The Clash for what
they've become, but that's not on,
talking about Red Wedge, in his gold
chains and his soul boy socks. He's no
better.

**Chris Maund, Mighty Ballistics Hi-
Power, 1986.**

Paul Weller? ... he's like the kid at
school who was in remedial class, and
he'd 'ave spit between his two top teeth,
and then flick his cigarette over the
school fence as a sign of rebellion. It's
all very well maturin' at 26, but when
yer just maturin' into a fifth form
remedial, what's the point?

Ian McCulloch, 1984.

Let's talk about fucking Joe Strummer. When he went missing that time and they cancelled the tour, they found him in parlez-vous Francais having a holiday with a young kitty. How lovely! Joe, the kids are where it's at, right?! Hypocrite.

Johnny Rotten, 1982.

Boring old farts!

Belouis Some, on Red Wedge, 1986.

PIL sounds to me like Uriah Heep on mandrax.

Joe Strummer, The Clash, 1982.

. . . Joe Strummer in his designer combat gear, drawing his Samurai sword and looking into the sun. That's not being a hero, that's being a ham.

Chris Maund, Mighty Ballistics Hi-Power, 1986.

The Clash are a bunch of clapped-out old social workers.

Fred and Judy Vermorel, Sex Pistols' biographers, 1978.

The thing that pisses me off about the Clashes and Billy Braggs is that all they ever do is state the bleedin' obvious. All Billy Bragg's doing is telling people that Thatcher's a cow. Well, I think most people know that, don't they?!

Rat Scabies, 1985.

Time after time, they've fucked the working class, they've shit over them. They've introduced internment in Ireland, they brought the fuckin' troops over, the fuckin' shipbuilders strike – they fuckin' smashed that, and you can turn around and *still* seriously support that party?

Ivor Perry, Easterhouse, on the Labour Party, 1986.

I don't hate Roy Hattersley, but he's the person I *dislike* the most.

Kim Wilde, makes an interesting distinction, 1987.

You can't trust politicians. It doesn't matter to me who makes a political speech. It's all lies . . . and it applies to any rock star who wants to make a political speech as well.

Bob Geldof, 1978.

The kids understand he's a knob-head.

Ian McNab, on Derek Hatton, 1986.

The only thing that could possibly save British politics, would be Margaret Thatcher's assassin.

Morrissey, 1984.

She's such a groupie, isn't she, Margaret Thatcher. She should be a pom-pom girl for Ronnie.

Mick Jones, B.A.D., 1987.

Let's put it this way – I wish she'd been in a different room at Brighton.

Shane MacGowan, The Pogues, 1985.

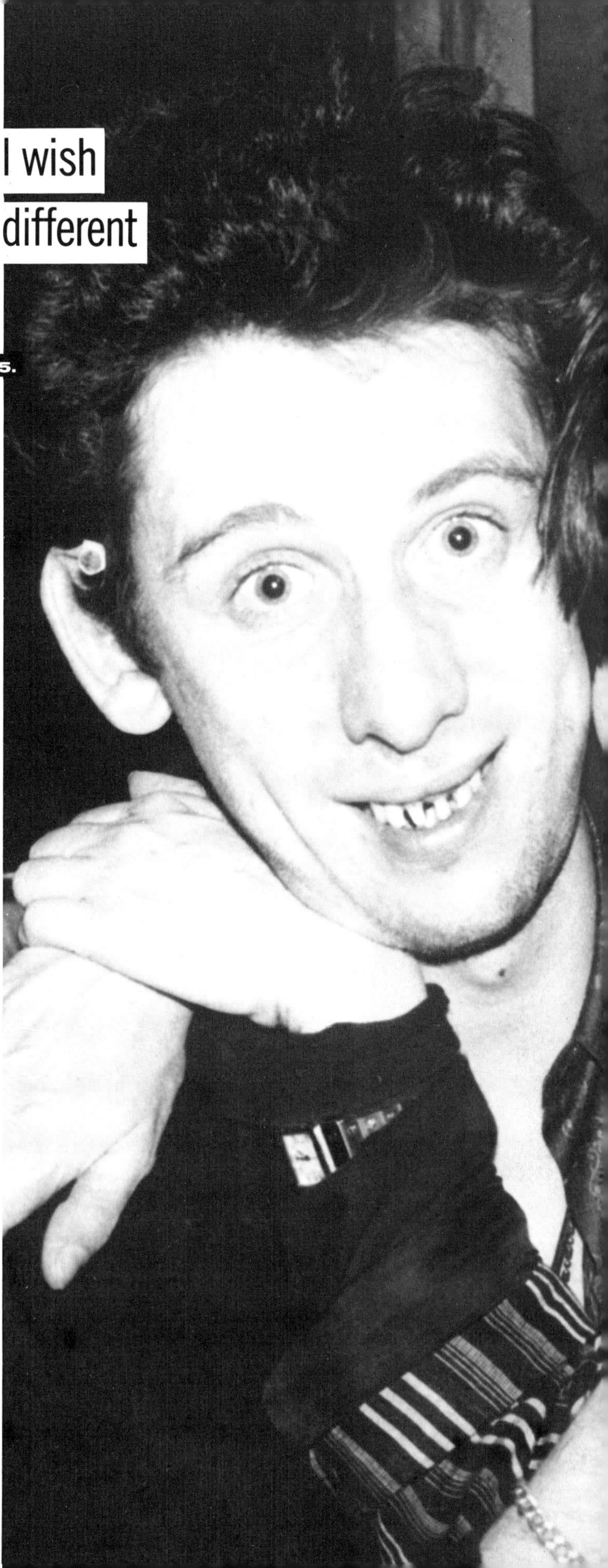

To vote conservative, you've just got to be a wanker!

Julian Cope, 1985.

I don't want to preach or be some bloody messiah. I don't ramble on and say I want everybody to hold hands and kiss one another, or any of that crap. So if I dedicate a song to Reagan I say, 'Greasy-haired git' – or if it's Thatcher I say, 'vile cow' . . . that's about it.

Terry Hall, The Specials, 1981.

They threw eggs at Thatcher in Glasgow – it was a waste of damn good eggs.

John Martyn, 1981.

Steven Wells asks, 'How come you don't see Christians on picket lines at Wapping, or outside the South African embassy?' I know of several Christians who've been at Wapping, and to say Christians aren't involved in the struggle against apartheid, is just crap! What I want to know is why I never see S. Wells or his friends The Redskins at Wapping? Too busy mouthing off?!!

A non-Christian, London, letter to the *NME*, 1986.

I'd visit her if she was in hospital on her deathbed – just to check she'd really gone.

D.C. Lee, on Margaret Thatcher, 1985.

There's a certain feeling in this country, that if you don't end up poor after starting out poor, then it's heresy.

Peter Stringfellow, club owner, 1986.

What would I buy Jeffrey Archer for Christmas? . . . A packet of three!

Stuart Adamson, Big Country, 1987.

Somebody must have voted for Thatcher.

Jim Kerr, Simple Minds, 1984.

I'd probably butt the cunt all over the golf-course, the Tory traitor!

Pete Wylie, on a proposed meeting with fellow Liverpudlian Jimmy Tarbuck, 1987.

The most horrific statement that I heard recently was Arthur Scargill when he said that we're not fighting for our jobs, we're fighting for our children's jobs. Bloody hellfire, I'm glad I'm not his son. Who wants to go down the mines in this beautiful age of possibilities?

Peter Stringfellow, 1986.

To be honest with you, I think that the working-class are as bigoted and conservative as the other classes anyway. In fact the working-class mentality is pretty stupid.

Graham Parker, 1978.

Why is Reagan there? I'm sure this is a question that's even foxing Americans. It's the 'Daz' mentality. I'm sure they'd elect Joan Collins if she were available!

Morrissey, 1985.

The LP 'Gracelands', of course, is the ultimate evidence of a guy with his head firmly up his rectum when it comes to political analysis . . . Whatever else he is – ace songwriter, Afro-American music pioneer (cough), good guy out to lunch in the real world – Paul Simon is, always has been and always will be, a product of the West Coast school of endless introversion.

Calvin Hobbes, journalist, 1988.

I'd rather talk to Nigel Dempster than some boring union official.

Bryan Ferry, 1984.

I saw Elton John on the telly saying that he was gonna play in South Africa. That really makes me sick. He may not realise it but, by going over there, he's giving the South African government a real one-up. It's a great propaganda exercise for them when people like him go and play there.

Jerry Dammers, 1984.

Art Garfunkel makes Paul Simon look like LL Cool J.

Ian Gittins, journalist, 1988.

I did a pop quiz with Jon Moss from Culture Club, and we were making small talk. He was talking about the fact that he'd never buy a fur coat for anybody. He thought it was digusting. I said to him that I thought his opinions about that clashed greatly with his opinions about other things, because he was very pro nuclear arms. And I said to him, 'You know, I'm confused, are you right-wing, left-wing, or are you just not bothered?' And then I saw two or three interviews with him in the next month where he referred to this very same conversation and said that I'd turned round to him and said, 'oh you're so right-wing' – and he said that I was just a trendy young left-winger. I was so fucking cross, I said if I ever lay eyes on that bloke again, I'll knock his head off!

Tracie Young, 1985.

When one looks at all the individuals within the Royal Family, they're so magnificently, unaccountably boring! I mean, Diana herself has never in her lifetime uttered one statement that has been of any use to any member of the human race. The whole thing seems like a joke, a hideous joke. We don't believe in Leprechauns, so why should we believe in the Queen.

Morrissey, 1986.

A piece of cardboard that they drag round on a trolley.

Johnny Rotten, on the Queen, 1977.

Thatcher is the mouthpiece of a whole ideology which should be exterminated.

Kirk Brandon, 1984.

How can you possibly believe in the tooth-fairy with a conservative government?

Robert Smith, The Cure, 1985.

I think the whole thing of politics is a load of crap, so don't bother to vote – shoot people. That's my message kids!

James King, 1985.

I think the dole rate in Britain is horribly low . . . unless you've got nine fucking horrible kids. You should get £35, whereas a guy who's got fucking eight kids, who's totally irresponsible – like, he can't even use a durex! – gets £200 a week. The guy's a dick, y'know, he should be punished for that.

Mark E. Smith, 1986.

I'd emphasise we're what I'd consider to be a fairly nice bunch of blokes and

definitely not very violent people either, but *they* inspire the most violent reaction in me. I think they're just *totally* unreasonable, *totally* out of order – their unreasonableness is *absolute*. There isn't a single excuse for them . . .

Paul Heaton, The Housemartins, on the Royal Family, 1986.

They are grotesquely ugly people . . . They're like people you don't wanna meet . . . ever. It's just their whole attitude stinks, all their Fred Perry shirts, y'know. It's all condescending to me. And *Hull*, Hull is a *horrible* place.

Mark E. Smith, The Fall, on The Housemartins, 1986.

The Housemartins?!! I couldn't acknowledge them as the competition without a smile on my face.

Johnny Marr, on The Smiths' reign, 1987.

The system want pure love songs like ol' Frank Sinatra, they do't want not'ing wit' no protest. It makes too much trouble.

Bob Marley, 1978.

You know, when it's publicly stated that policemen aren't racist, it's so ludicrous I don't even bother to laugh.

David Grant, Linx, 1981.

I find politics ruins everything. Music, films, it gets into everything and fucks it all up. People need more sense of humour.

Grace Jones, 1985.

We've had about 10 years of rotten musicians quoting the same line from Nietzsche: 'What doesn't destroy me strengthens me.' The West absorbs all dissidents. We've all watched generation upon generation of disaffected teenagers being acknowledged by the establishment, and used as proof of their flexibility and continued viability. Anything that doesn't bring down the system, strengthens it. You can't *sing* South Africa to death.

Robert Wyatt, 1984.

Rock 'n' roll is a way of life – meaning acid, Woodstock, the Maharishi, and police brutality.

Pete Townshend, 1972.

I hate American cops. They seem to be in it for the money. That's one thing about keeping the money down here, at least the police are in it for a vocation. Once money gets involved it destroys everything.

Eric Burdon, 1966.

Rock music is at the stage where it has become part of the establishment . . . How can you be a rebel, when rebellion is the norm? Therefore rock 'n' roll has lost its power as a revolutionary force. I think the bands who call themselves revolutionary are playing at it. They're having no effect whatsoever.

Sting, 1982.

Sting was boring and pretentious. Everyone was driven to distraction by his endless speeches on political matters.

Kathleen Turner, actress, on her *Julia Julia* co-star, 1988.

It didn't make artistic sense. The Smiths are more important than The Police! We're more important than they ever were, or ever will be.

Johnny Marr, on his group's refusal to tour with The Police, 1984.

I have no faith in politics, and place no value in leadership of any kind.

Sting, 1981.

People just come up to me and say, 'I think you're shit' – so I say, 'I may be shit, but at least I'm successful and making money at shit, whereas you're just shit'– ha-ha!

Marc Almond, 1982.

Money is a constantly draining occupation – trying to deal with it, keep it, get it. I find the business side very distasteful, harrowing and soul destroying. I could talk about tax, which I find quite frightening. But this always sounds like a soft and phoney complaint . . . I do get the sense, though, that it's illegal to earn money in this country.

Morrissey, 1988.

Mike Oldfield must be a very rich bloke by now. I think he should change his name to Mike *Oilfield*.

Andy Taylor, letter to the *Melody Maker*, 1976.

All money is a waste of money.

Mark E. Smith, 1985.

The picture of America you're presented with here, is really prejudicial and incorrect. They're not like that – they're worse!

Johnny Rotten, 1983.

You've got to see America for what it is – the most disgusting country in the world.

Ian McCulloch, 1983.

A toss-pot is even lower than a jerk-off. A weed is a pansy. If you don't know that, it's just an indication of how fucking stupid you Americans are.

Johnny Rotten, 1977.

Los Angeles is supposed to be like this sunny paradise, and all the palm trees are covered in smog. The sun's just a blur above the smog. We looked at the Hollywood Hills, and they're just scum. It's like Huddersfield. You could wipe your finger on the hill and there'd be dust on it.

Ian McCulloch, 1981.

Los Angeles is awful – like Liverpool with palm trees.

Johnny Rotten, 1987.

You cowboys are all faggots.

Sid Vicious, to Texas audience, 1978.

LA's okay I guess, if you wanna be the bronzed Goddess, driving around in your Cherokee jeep, in your satin shorts, with your ass-hole jerk-off rock 'n' roll star boyfriend, with his shorts full of cocaine . . .

Chrissie Hynde, The Pretenders, 1981.

When we played the 'Whiskey-A-Go-Go' in Los Angeles we were received with hip contempt, aggressive apathy, as if to say they'd seen it all before. But they hadn't, because they hadn't seen us. Afterwards, Ray Manzarek came into the dressing room. I was sitting on the floor, knackered, trying to get some kip, and he said, 'Hello Mac' . . . I looked at him and it was obvious who he was. No-one else is quite that bad looking.

Ian McCulloch, 1981.

New York is just one big Dingwalls.

Johnny Rotten, 1978.

Urgh! LA!! The saddest, most plastic fantasy city . . . It's like everybody has been given a sedative!

Marc Almond, 1983

People talk about the Third World, you know, and they think the Third World is, like, *Guam* or somewhere. But I've seen the Third World man, and it ain't Guam. The Third World is Lawrence, Kansas.

Joe 'King' Carrasco, 1981.

New York? Who'd want to live there? It's like living on top of a rotting corpse, vampire life. You crawl out of your coffin and go into the decaying streets – and get shot at.

John Hiatt, 1982.

I'm not saying that Americans are models of perfection, but 'diseased Orang-Utans' is a little extreme. I'm sure they're a *couple* of steps up from that.

Morrissey, 1985.

When you're used to living in England, America is all the things that everyone says about it. The cities are filthy, the air is unbreathable, and in general the people are bloody rude. I certainly wouldn't entertain living there, and I certainly wouldn't want to bring up my daughter there.

Keith Moon, The Who, 1970.

I am so sick of everyone in England putting down America and everything about it! You don't live here and you ►

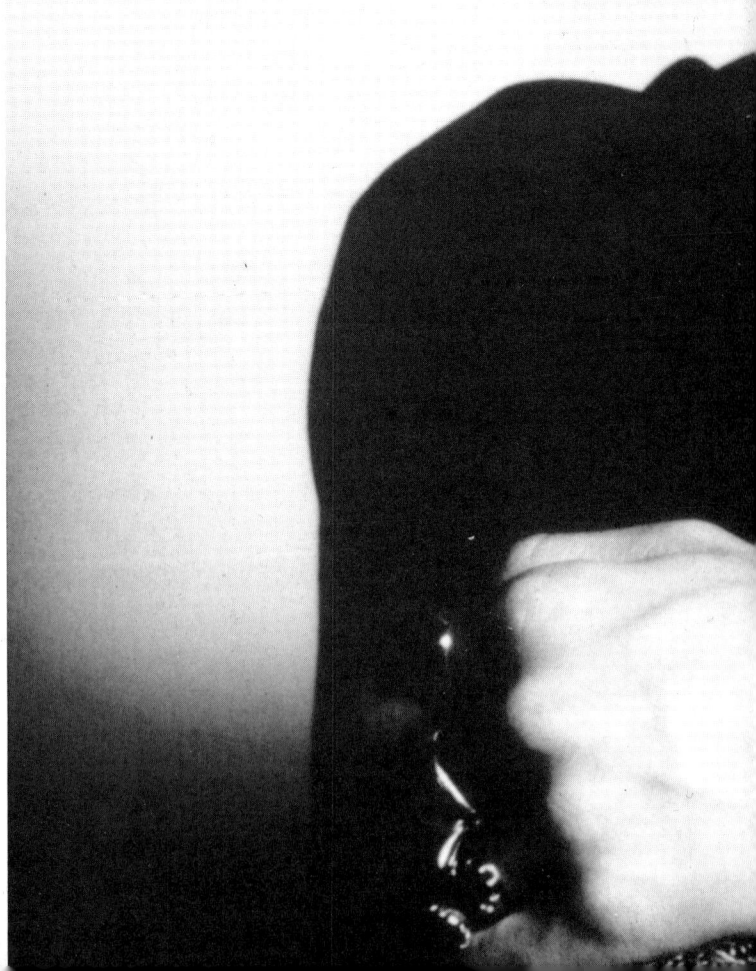

► don't know what it's really like . . . Your constant belittling of America makes you Brits seem like mindless idiots, which we have always suspected you were.

Lisa Lisa, letter to the *Melody Maker*, 1988.

England's *terrible*! It's got the worst air, the worst water, the worst food, the worst anything-you-wanna-name. It is the pits. Every single person in the whole country smokes cigarettes, and they all have brown teeth and rotted out gums. Everything is black from coal. The buildings are black, the streets are black, the signs are black. After you go there for two months you're wishing for the USA. You go crazy over there. We're big stars in England!

Fee Waybill, The Tubes, 1978.

English people are just as boorish and just as ignorant abroad as Americans. I've seen them and it's true.

Neil Peart, Rush, 1983.

I'm American, and when you travel the rest of the world you realise that, whatever America did, it did it right.

Sammy Hagar, 1986.

There's something frighteningly artificial about everything here – the whole place is geared up for tourism now. London's a kind of massive souvenir shop, a facade of how London used to be. It just isn't English any more. It seems very Americanised, which is something to dwell upon with horror.

Morrissey, 1983.

If anyone gives me a patriotic speech, I know he's an arsehole.

Joe Strummer, The Clash, 1982.

I don't like England very much these days. It's very depressing, there's no zap any more.

Roger Taylor, Queen, 1979.

Queen are more to be pitied than blamed.

Steve Sutherland, journalist, 1984.

I said to my boyfriend Arnie, 'Ya gotta kiss me where it smells' – so he drove me to Wapping.

Bette Midler, 1978.

It takes years to break America. In England you just have to look cute and dress well.

John Waite, 1984.

America has been looking for somewhere to put the Vietnam war for

so long. We're making movies to help us forget . . . The budget for *Rambo* was so many millions of bucks, and here's this guy with all his muscles and a big machine gun. But the veterans were treated like dogmeat. The film budget was so many millions of dollars and they get 100 dollars a month.

Tom Waits, 1985.

Most people seem to have an inferiority complex and think America is better, which is an amazing result of post-war brainwashing, because everyone knows that Americans have got smaller brains. Fact of life, you know – they're just inferior specimens.

Jean Jacques Burnel, The Stranglers, 1978.

Aurrrrrrgh!! What was that I was drinking last night!?! My head feels like there's a Frenchman living in it.

Rowan Atkinson, comedian, 1988.

I'm bored stiff with people complaining about the French and never going there,

or just going to the obvious places. They have no concept of what the French are at all. I do . . . and they are *awful*!!

Johnny Rotten, 1986.

I remember Brian Epstein best for a story that may or may not be true. In his mansion he kept *Spanish* servants, none of whom could speak any English. Let that be a lesson to us all in discretion.

Lou Reed, on the deceased Beatles manager, 1967.

You know what the Italians are like . . . fucking chaos!

Johnny Rotten, 1983.

Any country that can be invaded by the Italians, must be a right load of crap.

Mark E. Smith, 1986.

I can't think of a single thing I'd like to say about Sweden. Scandinavia . . . I mean, how the hell can you get so much boredom into a song? It'd be so depressing people would kill themselves. Two minutes of complete silence would sum it up.

Johnny Rotten, 1977.

I *could* go to Japan after a year, but I think it would probably be more fun to play somewhere elsc!

Paul McCartney, 1980.

Belgium? Hated it. No time for the Belgians. Almost as bad as the bleedin' Swiss. Nation of money-grabbin' clockmakers.

Nick Lowe, 1978.

You fly in, you've had some crap on the 'plane, and all you wanna do is have a look around, send a few postcards home . . . but you get pushed into a studio and someone says, *'Ere*, do nutty skanks, nutty dis, zany zany, nutty, great!' And you think, 'Fucking hell, can't wait to get home' – know what I mean?

Chas Smash, Madness, in Holland, 1981.

I mean, Venezuela – is it going to be full of Aztecs, or what? . . . Why can't we tour places where they speak English and serve decent beer?

Terry Chambers, XTC, 1981.

I'd like to play in Russia and I'd like to play in China. I think it should have been The Style Council who played over there – not Wham!

Paul Weller, 1985.

By and large, Australian men are a horrible breed.

Robert Foster, The Go-Betweens, 1986.

Australian pop? . . . As fizzy as Fosters.

As jumpy as a kangaroo. As original as sherbert. As lively as a dead wombat!

***Sounds* editorial, 1982.**

Old punks don't die, they make it big in the US.

Simon Hills, journalist, 1982.

There was a time when the idea of Billy Idol one day becoming a megaplatinum punk-rock superstar would have made me choke on my nutburger . . .

Mat Snow, journalist, 1984.

Is this man a prat?

Headline to Freddie Mercury feature, *NME*, 1977.

Is this man a prat?

Billy Idol picture caption, *NME*, 1984.

Boy George once called me a head without a brain, and Johnny Rotten always called me the Perry Como of punk. But so what?!

Billy Idol, 1986.

Billy Idol has made two or three good records, but when he opens his mouth he's still a prat.

Tony James, 1986.

WHATEVER HAPPENED TO BLOATED ROCK STARS?

Headline to Billy Idol feature, *NME*, 1984.

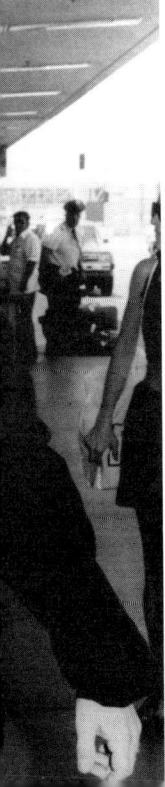

The record company wanted me to brush down my hair like David Cassidy. I said, 'Sod off!'

Billy Idol, 1984.

All major record company press officers have a baked bean for a brain.

Chris Roberts, journalist, 1988.

You go into a record company press office these days and they start talking to you about 'the psychology of the music business'. Goddammmm. What have we got to do with any of that? We jes' play the blues. You don't go to a fuckin' psychiatrist for dancing lessons, so how come they're talking all this psychology shit to us?

Kim Wilson, Fabulous Thunderbirds, 1981.

Richard Branson's got ridiculously enormous teeth. One day all these cretins with big teeth and long hair and cheesecloth shirts started turning up at our gigs. These people were from Virgin Records.

Andy Partridge, XTC, 1978.

It's getting to the lazy stage, where people simply present a very flimsy piece of music and hand it to Nile Rodgers or Bill Laswell to go away and work magic with.

Alan, Chakk, 1984.

They're quite the commune, Virgin Records. A load of groupies as secretaries . . . all Hampstead hippies.

Johnny Rotten, 1978.

Motown was the sixties, and that's the problem with Motown. They think they're still *in* the sixties. They're not, and they gotta cater for the people in the street. All the old Supremes fans are winos with false teeth.

Rick James, 1984.

Sometimes we lose our temper with people like record company executives or whatever. I often feel like slapping them around the face.

Brian Johnson, AC/DC, 1983.

I consider most producers wankers.

Phil Collen, Def Leppard, 1983.

This one's for all you A & R men at the bar.

Siouxsie Sioux, introducing 'Hong Kong Garden' at The Music Machine, 1978.

Like his last one, this tends
to provoke cries of 'Heap of shit'
– until you've heard
it five times, whereupon
you confess that it's
preferable to *anything* by
George Harrison.

**Sandy Robertson, journalist,
reviewing Paul McCartney's
'Waterfalls', 1980.**

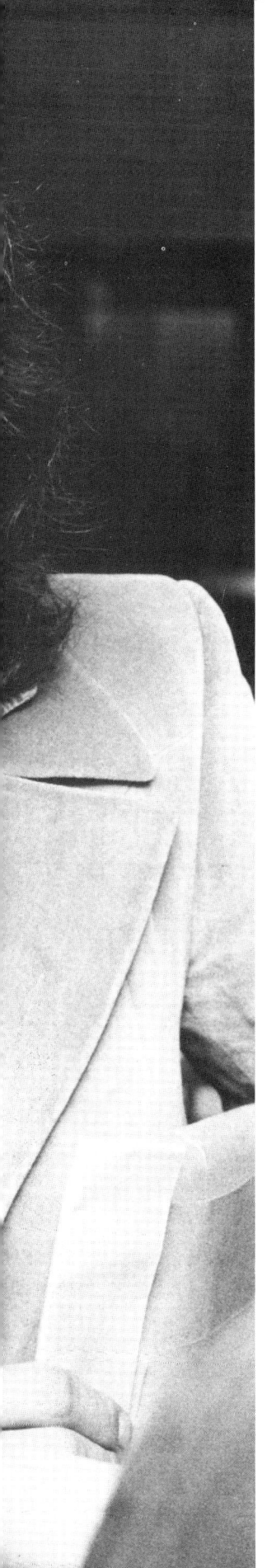

My attitude to The Banshees is rather more fragmented than theirs. I beat them at pool. They get ratty.

Robert Smith, The Cure, 1983.

Sid decided some time ago that he was going to become an arsehole, and he did.

Johnny Rotten, 1978.

Our gig in Huddersfield on Christmas Day was brilliant. A benefit for striking foremen and orphans and things like that . . . I was pushed into a Christmas cake by a load of horrible six-year-old girls. Savage beasts. That was great. So good. Sid was pinching sweets from everyone. He couldn't cope at all with having kids for an audience. Just couldn't handle it. He couldn't do all that nonsense with his shirt off and his face. It didn't wash at all. They just thought he was a buffoon. And he knew they knew. And he was.

Johnny Rotten, 1978.

Sid Vicious is the greatest rock 'n' roll bass player in the world. I know, 'cos I taught him everything.

Captain Sensible, 1978.

The reputation Sid got for himself as a bass player! Johnny Thunders . . . now, you know what he's like. He's out of his box. He refused to let Sid jam with him because he thinks Sid is so appalling it's not worth talking about. I thought that was so funny – one junkie being discerning about another.

Johnny Rotten, 1978.

John's just jealous because I'm the brains of the group. I've written all the songs, even from the beginning when I wasn't even in the group. They were so useless they had to come to me because they couldn't think of anything by themselves.

Sid Vicious, 1977.

Only very recently – when they realised that the publishing money was involved – have the other members of the band come up with ideas for songs.

Bob Geldof, on his Boomtown Rats, 1978.

Trouble is, there's a gap of a decade between each good song.

Morrissey, on Lou Reed, 1984.

I've worked me bloody way into the **record business**, and now I've got **teachers again**, slapping me wrists **every time I** don't quite pull it off.
Paul McCartney, 1978.

Even now, I don't think there's anyone in **rock 'n' roll** who's writing lyrics that **mean anything**, other than ME.
Lou Reed, 1978.

Was Ringo's nose as large as legend has it?
Gary Crowley, prize pillock, 1984.

The Beatles never had anything to say. It was always nice happy stuff. What *did* they ever say?
Lou Reed, 1973.

Do I think The Beatles pose a threat to Tears For Fears? Naaah, one of them's dead.
Roland Orzabel, Tears For Fears, 1985.

Paul McCartney is a dope, because he smokes too much cannabis . . . I think he sees himself as becoming a kind of hero because of all his busts and the way he has made a stand for legalisation. Personally, I wish he'd just stop being so silly.
Denny Laine, 1984.

The fans regarded Paul as their property. They were furious that their innocent, wholesome little idol had been caught by a woman who was everything nice girls aren't – divorced with a small child, working for her living and totally unglamorous. She even had the audacity to be American!
Johnny Waller, journalist, on Linda McCartney, 1984.

When Pete Townshend wrote 'My Generation' he wasn't speaking for himself or his public. He was just taking the piss out of Roger Daltrey, 'cos he thought he was thick.
Jerry Dammers, 1980.

Imagine crossing a Darts audience with a Bob Dylan crowd, and you get an idea of a Wings concert. Family entertainment from a living legend.
Penny Kiley, journalist, 1979.

I've already forgotten who Bob Dylan was.
Elvis Costello, 1978.

We toured America for 10 weeks with Elvis Costello. He's just a little fuckin' arsehole . . . I didn't waste two words talking to him throughout those 10 weeks, man.
Willy De Ville, 1978.

If ever there was a time to be unfashionable, this is it. If people want to buy records by groups like Spandau Ballet and Echo And The Bunnymen, then fuck them. They don't deserve any better.

Elvis Costello, 1981.

I don't think Elvis Costello is any better than me. That's such a ludicrous thing for anyone to think.

Graham Parker, 1978.

Elton John and Elvis Costello – these are the kind of guys who, if they sat next to you at high school, you wouldn't talk to because they were creeps. Costello's image is so totally *unindividual* – Mr Ordinary – yet he can pass it off as being unique. I don't know the guy, so I don't know if he's sincere. I don't even know if he's for real. My tendency is to believe that he's not for real. I can't believe in a guy who's coming on and playing a ripped-off buncha shit from 10 years ago.

Tom Verlaine, 1978.

I don't like people like Rod Stewart and Elton John, and I don't like the way they carry on. I get very upset at being identified with that kind of person.

Mick Jagger, 1978.

If Rod Stewart comes back to Britain, he's going to have a fight to earn his old mates back. You don't last long as a human being if you live his type of life.

Pete Townshend, 1977.

It's understandable to me, perhaps not to you, but I can only think of inconsequentially detrimental things to say about the emergence of lyrics from my various bodily orifices. 'Substitute', for example, was written as a spoof of 'Nineteenth Nervous Breakdown'. On the demo I sang with an affected Jagger-like accent which Kit (The Who's manager) obviously liked, as he suggested the song as a follow-up to 'My Generation'. The lyric has come to be the most quoted Who lyric ever. It somehow goes to show that the 'trust the art, not the artist' tag, that people put on Dylan's silence about his work, could be a good idea. To me, 'Mighty Quinn' is about the five Perfect Masters of the age, the best of all being Meher Baba of course. To Dylan, it's probably about gardening, or the joys of placing dog shit in the garbage to foul up Alan J Weberman.

Pete Townshend, 1970.

I don't give a monkey's willie.

Neil Arthur, Blancmange, 1984.

Pete Townshend half admits that he doesn't know what's happening on the streets. I don't think he ever knew.

Johnny Rotten 1977.

I feel sorry for Johnny Rotten, because he's a paranoid clown.

Hugh Cornwell, The Stranglers, 1976.

The Stranglers? . . . that group must take the biscuit for really not knowing anything.

Pete Townshend, 1977.

A record to make The Stranglers cult heroes with Julio Iglesias fans.

Colin Irwin, journalist, on 'Golden Brown', 1982.

The Who and The Stones are revolting. All they're good for is making money.

Johnny Rotten, 1986.

Jagger was standing outside the shop for hours trying to work up the bottle to come in, and after about three hours he decided to risk it and chance a look around. All that time to work up his bottle, and then I slammed the door in his face. Pathetic old bastard.

Johnny Rotten, 1977.

That bit about Johnny Rotten slamming the door in me face outside of Malcolm McLaren's *Sex* shop, is a lot of rubbish. He only says all those nasty bits about me 'cause he loves me so much . . . I don't even know where the *Sex* shop is . . . Hold on, I vaguely recall where *Let It Rock* used to be. But there's a lot of clothes shops in the Kings Road. They all know I'm the only one who's got any money to spend on their crappy clothes . . . though even I would draw the line on spending money on torn T-shirts.

Mick Jagger, 1977.

I touched Mick Jagger. Honest! Down the Wag Club. I was there with Josie and she says 'Mick Jagger has just come in' and I says, 'C'mon, no way!' But when I turned round it's *him*, so I rush over and prod him in the stomach and he steps back, y'know, all stiffening and he nearly shits and I think 'Uh, oh!' And I'm losing me bottle, y'know, 'cos he's probably thinking 'Gun, John Lennon,' y'know. So I says, 'It's okay, I only wanted to touch you' and he gives me *that* smile, turns round and leaves. Just like that. Complains on the way out that he's been *harassed*...

Pete Wylie, 1984.

The Rolling Stones are The Shadows plus 2,000 decibels. And I never did think much of The Shadows.

Tommy Steele, 1976.

I despise stars. They're bullshit people. They live in their rich mansions, fucking completely out of touch with reality. They know nothing about real people any more. They're just drugged-out arseholes.

Johnny Rotten, 1977.

John Lennon ain't no revolutionary – he's a fucking idiot.

Todd Rundgren, 1975.

If I found her floating in my pool, I'd punish my dog.

Joan Rivers on Yoko Ono, 1983.

If you believe in rock stars you're just gonna be disappointed, y'know. It's like, when I was 12 or 13 I had all these rebel idols like The Stones, and at that age you really idolise them, you really think they're kicking authority in the teeth just by having the nerve to *be* The Stones. Then you turn around and you find Mick

Jagger hanging around with, like, Princess Margaret. I mean, what's the point. You can't idolise people like that, it's just desperate.

Johnny Marr, 1984.

Robert Plant came down The Roxy surrounded by millions of bodyguards. One of them came up to me and said, 'Robert Plant wants to talk to you, now you aren't gonna start anything are you?' And all these heavies are around me waiting for me to have a go at him. And he's twice my fucking size! What am I going to do? I just looked at him, and he's like a real ignorant old northerner, and I felt really sorry for him. Now, how can you respect someone like that?

Johnny Rotten, 1977.

Don Johnson . . . wins the Eddie Murphy prize for milking celebrity as far as it will go.

Helen Fitzgerald, journalist, 1986.

Bands like Yes and Pink Floyd make records which they know will please their public. Bands like that are enemies of mine. They really are retards. They're not achieving anything. They've got all their equipment and all that money, and they do sod all. They stay in ►

Iggy Pop?!? ... Musically he's *so* bad. I don't need to go and listen to a saw-mill all night!

► their own narrow-minded, whimsical, pathetic little ways, and never improve themselves or other people!

Johnny Rotten, 1981.

He's a miserable sod.

Glen Matlock, The Sex Pistols, on Johnny Rotten, 1977.

Dull as old dishwater.

Helen Fitzgerald, journalist, on The Pretenders, 1984.

Don't you think Siouxsie looks like Elizabeth Taylor . . .? Well, I do.

Boy George, 1983.

How can you respect somebody who's still not learnt to play a second string on his bass? It doesn't mean I think he's a talentless turd, 'cos I think that Siouxsie And The Banshees are brilliant, but he has played the same bass-line for the last 10,000 years!

Pete Burns, Dead Or Alive, on Steve Severin, 1984.

He's like a *lesser* Eric Clapton.

Chris Spedding, on Jimmy Page, 1976.

Some people don't know how to grow old gracefully.

Alan Lewis, journalist, on Chris Spedding, 1977.

I think Cliff Richard is controversial. Anyone who's lived with his mum for that long is definitely suspicious.

Johnny Rotten, 1986.

Old, ugly, escaped lunatics, dumb, aggressive.

Market research report on The Motors, 1978.

How nauseating, nasty and fascist is the new Motors advert. It depicts Jayne Mansfield saying, 'I lost my head over the Motors!'

Susan Stein, letter to the *NME*, 1977.

Far from being offensive, I think 'Too Drunk To Fuck' was an educational song. It's exactly the sort of thing that your mammy or Sunday School won't tell you about. I think the people banning the record are the people that it's happened to.

Jello Biatra, The Dead Kennedys, 1981.

Dead Kennedys – too clever to be genuine punk, not clever enough to be anything else.

Sounds editorial, 1982.

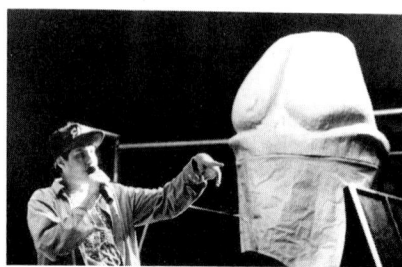

If anyone is offended by our records, it's because they're too stupid to listen.

Mike D, The Beastie Boys, 1987.

If people don't like what I do – fuck 'em.

Chris Hillman, 1977.

When you're young you want to be a footballer. When you're older you want to be in a pop group. It takes less talent.

Skin, Hipsway, 1986.

British football is so mundane, because everyone's influenced by midfield players instead of being influenced by George Best.

Johnny Marr, 1985.

Why should people pay money to stand in the cold and get beaten up by skinheads just to watch football, especially Bryan Robson and all those pissy players England have got?

England are the worst footballers in the world. I mean, Ray Wilkins and Graham Roberts . . . and Mark Hately playing centre-forward for England! Average talents.

Bobby Bluebell, 1984.

Bobby Charlton? Well, it's all psychological isn't it? He still thinks he's got it, but the parting's getting further and further down.

Errol Brown, on a sporting baldy, 1984.

I hate Terry Venables for the way he went on about National Service. He fucked off to Spain for the money, and then he comes up with all the answers. Twat.

Mark E. Smith, on a sporting know-it-all, 1985.

The pop star syndrome isn't what I want at all. Then you're just an empty vessel, a face, a lump of flesh.

Marc Almond, 1983.

I'd rather build boats. At least you can see what you've achieved at the end of it. In pop, all values are inflated and warped . . . In pop, nobody ever admits their ignorance. They've always got an answer for everything. In pop, you never hear anyone say, 'I don't know' . . .

Les Pattinson, 1985.

Music is like being a bank clerk.

Kate Bush, 1978.

Music is but a solitary turd in the sewer of existence.

Roger, Essex, letter to *Sounds*, 1977.

I hear musicians moaning about how hard they work and I think, oh fuck you, go get a *real* job. I mean, I'm technically working right now, talking to you, and how hard is this? Not very . . . Show me a guy with 50 million dollars who ain't happy, and I'll show you a fool.

Blackie Lawless, WASP, 1986.

There are times when being a workaholic, a perfectionist and an asshole really pays off.

Jane Simon, journalist, on Blackie Lawless, 1986.

Why does a man of appreciable wit and intelligence choose to portray himself as little more than a grunting Neanderthal?

The Stud Brothers, journalist(s), on Blackie Lawless, 1986.

The difference between us and Grateful Dead, is we work our arses off. Why go and see Grateful Dead live when you can sit at home, put their record on, get a poster with a fan underneath . . . and you'll see more movement than you ever did out of Jerry Garcia!?!

Blackie Lawless, 1984.

A lot of groups are so cheap – do things in such a cheap way. Obvious things. Like how many nights they can fill Hammersmith Odeon, things like that. As if it's important. They are all aiming for showbiz. It's important not to try and impress people. People who come to see you should try to impress *you*. I've been reading about groups (like Spandau) who can't sleep the night before the chart positions are released. It's pathetic.

Terry Hall, 1984.

I don't know what's happened to Terry Hall – he's just changed. You expect some of the audience not to get the point of what you're doing, but when the lead singer of the group doesn't get the point . . .

Jerry Dammers, on his one-time Specials colleague, 1983.

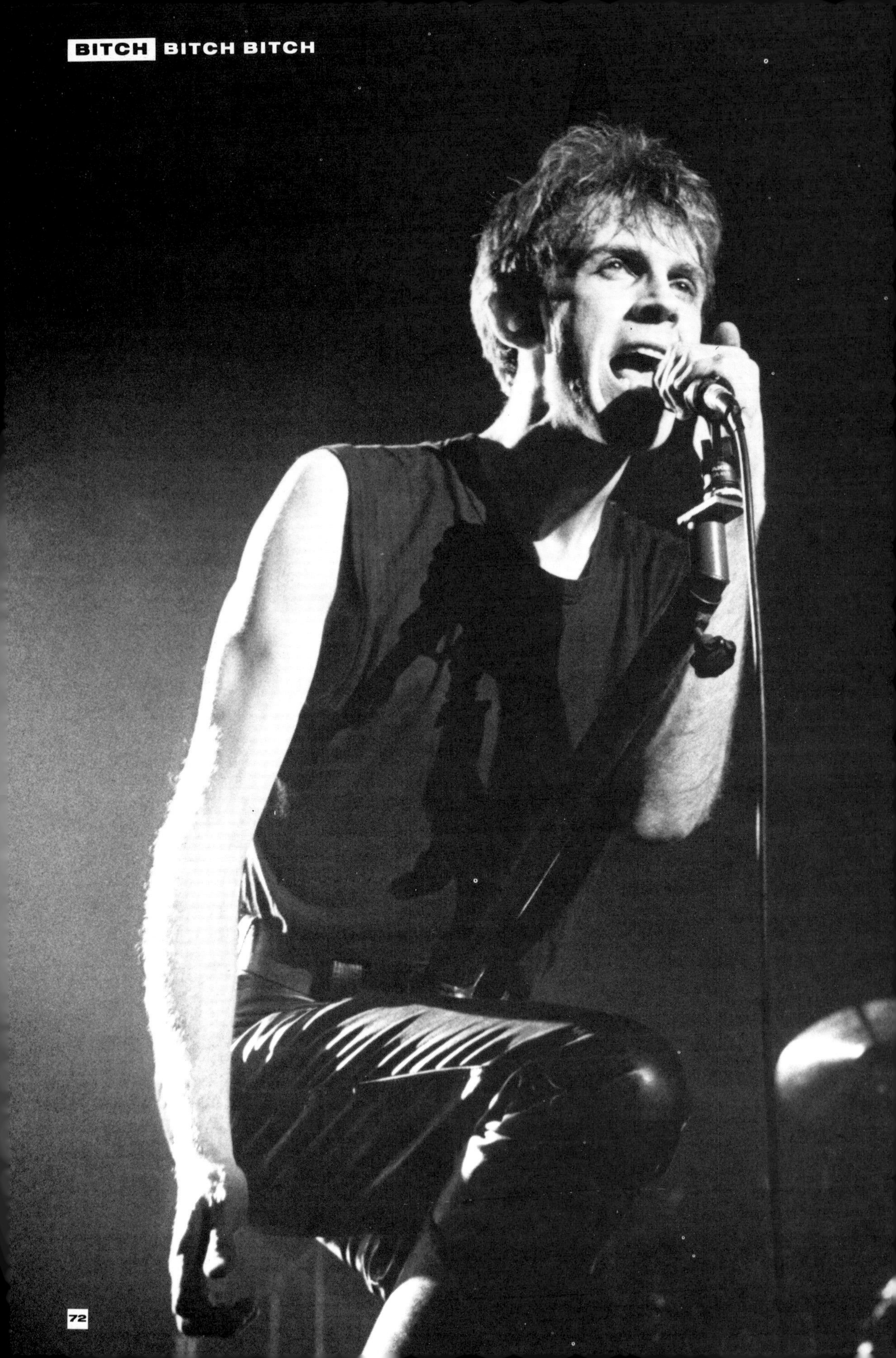

Julian Cope is like something
out of the Beano.

Ian McCulloch, 1983

He's really bitter now, and I don't know why. Maybe because he *did* want to be successful. He accuses us of compromising, of selling-out. We've never done that, but I remember *he* used to do gigs just for the money. And *that* is a sell-out when you listen to what he says . . . There's a joke from somebody in Liverpool: the most well-balanced person in the world has a chip on both shoulders. That's what Mark E. Smith is like now.

Ian McCulloch, 1984.

That's a conscious decision to buy clothes like that. I bet Mark Smith's got a wardrobe full of those Mark Smith shirts.

Ian McCulloch, 1981.

I went back to his house and his bedroom was just like what you'd expect. There were about 40 albums stacked against a radiator, about half of them were warped by the heat and they were *exactly* the right records for Mark Smith. And looking at his collection of shirts – *they* were exactly what you'd expect him to have!

Julian Cope, 1981.

Julian Cope's a fucking lunatic. Completely obsessed. Like the way he used to come round my house and rummage through my wardrobe, then go away and tell people all about it. I don't like that.

Mark E. Smith, 1988.

The man with the gum tree in his eyes.

Jonh Wilde, journalist, on Jonathan Richman, 1988.

Everyone says, 'Yeah George Michael, I know he's a bastard but he can write songs, and he arranges them too!' I think, what's the point? You can dress up a turd so much, but it still looks like a turd.

Julian Cope, 1985.

Wham! make me ill. It's not just the music, but the whole industry that surrounds them. All those poor kids in expensive shorts and shirts trying to be healthy. You go into a club and everybody looks as if they've been spreading Bisto gravy over their legs to make themselves brown.

Pete Wylie, 1984.

If you want to be Mr and Mrs Slob, fine. But don't bother coming to the Hippodrome.

Peter Stringfellow, club owner, 1986.

I really wanted to be Michael Jackson when I was growing up. But if I met him ➤

▶ today, I'd unplug his oxygen tent, rip off his surgical mask and spit in his face.

Mike D, The Beastie Boys, 1987.

We never did fit into that Tramps scene. We tried it, but we'd say, 'Quid for a drink? Piss off!'

Jim Lea, Slade, 1981.

Disco music doesn't exist as far as I'm concerned. Not to even a minuscule degree. I can't fathom Michael Jackson at all.

Morrissey, 1984.

The Beastie Boys are just dicks. Being successful won't change them. They'll always be dicks.

Russell Simmons, manager of The Beastie Boys, 1987.

If you wanna sell records, I'm told you gotta make videos. I know they're thought of as an art form, but I don't think they are . . . I've never known what anybody's doing with me. They filmed me from 30 yards away – what are they looking at? When I saw the video all I saw was a shot of me from my mouth to my forehead on the screen. I figure, isn't that something? I'm *paying* for that?

Bob Dylan, 1985.

When you make a video, you aren't in control. We wanted to keep it very simple, a straight performance. We explained what we wanted and everyone agreed that it would be fine. But you really don't know *what* they're filming. I said, 'Oh no, this is looking dodgy' – and they said, 'Ignore all those naked girls behind you, we're only filming your left hand!'

Ian Broudie, Care, 1984.

Pop video – you can go for weeks without seeing any adults.

NME editorial, 1985.

I don't know what pop videos are supposed to mean . . . video has had its day.

Mark E. Smith, The Fall, 1985.

People are still disturbingly vague about the treatment of animals. People still seem to believe that meat is a particular substance not at all connected to animals playing in the field over there. People don't realise how gruesomely and frighteningly the animal gets to the plate.

Morrissey, 1984.

You are what you eat, and who wants to be a lettuce?!!

Pete Burns, on vegetarians, 1984.

If make-up could come through on a record player, Kiss would have a huge hit.

Jet Black, The Stranglers, 1977.

People say we should be grateful to be in the charts. Would you be grateful to get your coat back from the cleaners when it belongs to you? I belong in the charts, and I'm not going to be grateful for it.

Pete Burns, Dead Or Alive, 1984.

It makes me mad, dickheads like 'im. I hope he doesn't get too badly injured in the car crash, you know.

Pete Wylie on Phil Oakey, Human League, 1983.

I'd *never* have worked for Woolworth's even if I hadn't joined The Human League.

Susanne, 1981.

The first time I was aware I was joining Bronski Beat was when I read it in the *Daily Mirror*.

Marc Almond, 1985.

They're awful people! They're horrible! They're trash!

Mick Jagger, on the British press, 1978.

The tabloids are there to be ridiculed. If only the general public understood that what you read in these things is utter garbage. A manipulation by extremely tedious, spiteful people. The gossip columnists of this world, they strike me as people who can't have sex, so they have this huge chip on their shoulder and everyone must suffer because of it. *Normal* people just wouldn't behave in that way.

Johnny Rotten, 1987.

The tabloids? . . . I just don't think people should co-operate with that medium of exposure. They're becoming more like pop papers than daily papers, and there's more important things to report than who's dancing with who at the opening of the Limelight.

Pete Burns, Dead Or Alive, 1987.

The Slimelight's alright. It's just the company you have to keep . . . a lot of turd-burglars, rear-gunners and fudge-packers

Johnny Rotten on London's Limelight Club, 1987.

Poor Fergie's bum! One paper said 'We can exclusively reveal that Fergie ate 12 chocolates' at some do. Who the fuck cares how many chocolates somebody eats?

Pete Burns, Dead Or Alive, 1987.

I don't talk to the *Sun*. I know they'll fabricate things anyway, but why make life easy for them?

Holly Johnson, 1986.

All the daily tabloids treat me as a dangerous figure and that pleases me. At least it means that I'm a strong person and I'm not Andrew Ridgeley.

Morrissey, 1984.

It's got to be your mother who's buying Wham! records for her little daughter, rather than serious people buying music. It's just a very lightweight image that seems to be reliant on a lot of nicey nicey things – like The Hollies.

Billy Idol, 1984.

Without the injection of my voice, you can forget The Hollies' *sound*.

Alan Clarke, 1973.

The climate that we're in now, competing with the likes of Randy Crawford, us slipping down the charts is like a compliment. Y'know, I thought

pop music was for young people, I thought it was to cause generation gaps, that's the most important thing. I mean, what are mums and dads for, but to rebel against.

Pete Burns, 1987.

Clap if we played something you came to hear.

Bob Dylan, to US audience, 1981.

God's a bit of a bore.

Billy Mackenzie, 1985.

Where *did* it all go wrong?

Allan Jones, journalist, on Bob Dylan's wavering popularity, 1988.

I don't like Bob Dylan. I don't like his attitude or his records. All he stands for is a bad influence. Being cheeky with the press was bad. He says he's not a singer – so why does he sing? If he's going to be a public figure, he's got to be in the press. All that protest thing was a load of rubbish. I don't *hate* listening to his records, but I can't stand it when people say he's a genius. I just want to forget about that fellow.

Tom Jones, 1966.

It's crap. Take it off . . . Hate these, trying to be comedy records when they're not even funny. There's nothing funny ►

I'm just not attracted to guys with beards. Maybe that's why Jesus bores me. Maybe if he shaved I'd dig him.

Patti Smith, 1977.

▶ about chips. I've heard this sort of thing since before the First World War! There are hundreds of people who *are* funny on record, but not this. Who is funny on record? Bob Dylan for one, ha-ha.

George Harrison, reviewing Barbara Kay's 'Chips With Everything', 1965.

Dylan once said to Keith, 'I could have written 'Satisfaction' but you couldn't have written 'Tambourine Man'.

Mick Jagger, 1968.

Brian Jones just seemed to deteriorate over the last couple of years of his life. So he wasn't *that* much of a loss, musically.

Bill Wyman, 1969.

Charlie Watts never could play a solo. And don't believe him when he says he only joined the band on a temporary basis, ha-ha. It was the only gig he could get.

Mick Jagger, 1978.

I think Patti Smith is crap. I think she's so awful . . . She's just full of rubbish. A *poseur* of the worst kind.

Mick Jagger, 1977.

Is Roy Orbison dead? Hard to tell these days, isn't it? Pop stars – they're dropping dead like flies. Dropping all over the place mate. I was in Turkey when Elvis choked it, by the way. They started playing all his records one after another, and eventually I sussed the logical thing – he'd snuffed it.

Mick Jagger, 1977.

Elvis Presley. Fuckin' good riddance to bad rubbish. I don't give a fuckin' shit, and nobody else does either. It's just fun to fake sympathy, that's all they're doing.

Johnny Rotten, 1977.

I don't think Sid (Vicious) would have liked being out there on Live Aid – shaking hands with Elton John.

Tony James, 1985.

The Sex Pistols are negative, nihilistic, ambition-less, and respect neither themselves, their customers, the media, their management, nor their record company. Then why do they expect to make a profit out of the British public?

Surely they wish to do just that – no-one forced them at gunpoint to sign with Virgin.

PJL, London, letter to *Sounds*, 1977.

I got a foul scent when Live Aid first occurred, and I still get the same smell. It's an inch away from Hollywood. When will the film appear, the solo LP is on the horizon, the book is here. It's bully boy tactics and dining out with royalty . . . and hearing Bob talk so lovingly about Prince Charles! To me, it's so unreal . . . I never mentioned the word 'greed'. If it had dealt with a domestic issue, I don't believe it would have received any attention whatsoever. If we talk about unemployment in England we're slapped across the face. I think there was something almost glamorous about the whole Ethiopian epic. In the first instance, it was far away, overseas. Pop stars, film stars. It was, and still is, escapism.

Morrissey, 1986.

That whole Ethiopian thing stinks. They're there, right, for better or for worse, but how can they bring a child into that knowing that the situation is gonna be there forever? How can they do it? Just for a fuck! They're filth – straight up.

Geordie, Killing Joke, 1986.

What they need is two tons of fucking birth pills.

Mark E. Smith, on the Ethiopian famine victims, 1985.

We weren't asked. Simple as that. I don't think we were considered important enough. What can I say . . . Let them starve!?

Jean Jacques Burnel, The Stranglers, on his group's non-attendance at Live Aid, 1985.

There was an incredible amount of wealth in the studio. People were singing, 'Feed The World', and saying it was the most worthwhile thing they'd ever done. And I thought, 'Did you actually do anything else about it?' I'll bet most of the people there didn't even go and buy the record.

George Michael, on Band Aid, 1985.

If most of those groups at Live Aid had donated their cocaine bills for a year, it would have saved as many lives. Basically, this business is totally corrupt and without morals, without principles, and it has no redeeming features. It's completely valueless. Live Aid hasn't changed that.

Chris Maund, Mighty Ballistics Hi-Power, 1986.

I never wanted Band Aid to go on for a long time. Then it would become an institution like *ICI* or the *NME*.

Bob Geldof, 1985.

Personally I blame Paula Yates for the new sedate Mick Jagger.

Boy George, on the mellowing of Bob Geldof, 1983.

For me Prince conveys nothing. The fact that he's successful in America is interesting simply because he's mildly fey and that hasn't happened before there. Boy George, again I think he doesn't really say anything either.

Morrissey, 1986.

It's funny though, because . . . everyone's going, 'Oh man, Prince has jammed with you!' and we're really supposed to be into it – and we just

think the geezer's one of the biggest wankers we've ever seen in our lives.

Jah Wobble, 1983.

Prince looks like a dwarf who's been dipped in a bucket of pubic hair.

Boy George, 1986.

If Prince came from Wigan he would have been slaughtered by now.

Morrissey, 1986.

You ain't no hero just because you get up on a stage.

Kirk Brandon, Spear Of Destiny, 1983.

I opened a show once for a guy called Buffalo Bob And The Howdy Dowdy Review. He was like an American children's programme host. We went out on a tour of colleges, and I'd have to do like three matinees for the children and their mothers. He used to call me 'Tommy' . . . I wanted to strangle the sonofabitch. I hoped he'd die of bone cancer the entire week.

Tom Waits, 1981.

The work 'Tommy' is such a pretentious piece of patchwork that one might overlook the fact that this melange of sound and fury, far from signifying nothing, actually resounds with more sinister moral imperatives. In addition to the blatant racism and sexism, *Tommy* projects the image of the visionary individual leader and the tortured masses yearning for the conformity of blind obeisance. It glorifies both sadism and masochism. And it encases this whole package in an anti-human metallic imagery whose favourite symbol is a steel ball-bearing. *Tommy* projects a culture based not on people, but androids, and while its progenitors might argue that they are only commenting on a world gone mad, they are actually normalising the values of fascism . . . Psychedelic drivel.

Irwin Silber, journalist, 1975.

I'm gonna stand up and get counted. I think fascism stinks. And I'm gonna go on stage and say so.

Pete Townshend, 1980.

The last piece of graffiti I saw was in the pub at the top o' my street. Over the toilet somebody had written: PETE TOWNSHEND IS A CAPITALIST PIG.

Pete Townshend, 1980.

All he knows is which curler to put on which side of his head.

Pete Townshend on Gary Glitter, 1976.

Steve Marriott's music falls short of potential . . . I don't like Yes . . . Jeff Beck is pathetic.

Pete Townshend, 1975.

He's talked himself up his own arse.

Roger Daltrey on Pete Townshend, 1975.

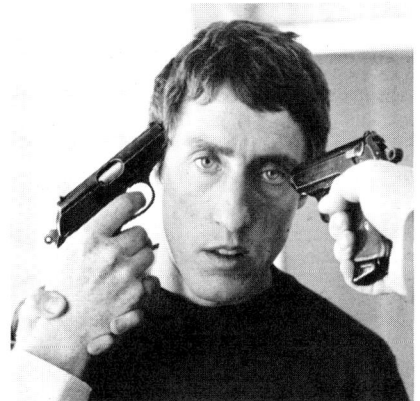

I lived the first four years after 'My Generation' in perpetual fear of getting kicked out of the band. They didn't want me in it . . . I think Townshend's always wanted to be me.

Roger Daltrey, 1975.

HI OUT THERE! Anyone still interested in a middle-aged Californian wife-beater?

Julie Burchill, journalist, forwarding an article on Bob Dylan, 1978.

This is an old Bob Dylan song which is dedicated to him because I want him to get better soon.

Kevin Coyne, introducing 'Knockin' On Heaven's Door' to US audience, 1981.

Who knows? Maybe you'll be around.

Bob Dylan, when asked by journalist Phillip Norman, whether the superstar wouldn't get bored on the film set of *Hearts Of Fire*, 1987.

If you want to sing about innocence or truth, or even God, nobody wants to know.

Bono, U2, 1983.

Leaning post.

Roy Harper, on religion, 1969.

How come nobody ever asks Kris Kristofferson questions like that?

Bob Dylan, when asked how he imagines God, 1976.

You don't watch someone die of Aids and still believe in God.

Diamanda Gallas, 1986.

You *know* no geezer is going to come down here and save you. That's just a myth propagated by churches and societies throughout history to subdue people . . . Don't be a fool, and you will have a future. If you want to be a cabbage, you might as well go to the supermarket with the rest of them and jump in the freezer.

Kirk Brandon, 1983.

The Catholic church has nothing in common with Christianity. I can remember being at school on a Monday and being asked, 'Did you go to church yesterday?' And if you hadn't been, you literally had your arms twisted off you. It's, 'We'll sever your head for your own good, my son'.

Morrissey, 1985.

I don't see why you have to go to church to pray. If you really believe in it, you should be able to pray anywhere – like all those really creepy born-again lot in America. Make me sick.

Paul Weller, 1985.

My so-called Jewish roots are in Egypt. They went down there with Joseph, and they came back out with Moses, you know, the guy that killed the Egyptian, married an Ethiopian girl and brought the law down from the mountain. The same Moses whose staff turned into a serpent. The same person that killed 3,000 Hebrews for getting down, stripping off their clothes and dancing around a golden calf.

These are my roots . . . Jacob had four wives and 13 children, who fathered an entire people. Those are my roots too. Gideon, with a small army, defeating an army of thousands. Deborah, the prophetess. Esther the queen and many Canaanite women. Reuben slipping into his father's bed when his father wasn't there. These are my roots. Delilah tempting Samson, killing him softly with her song. The mighty King David was an outlaw before he was a King, you know. He had to hide in caves and get his meals at back doors. The wonderful King Saul had a warrant out on him – a 'no knock' search warrant. They wanted to cut his head off. John The Baptist could tell you more about it. Roots man – we're talking about Jewish roots, you want to know more?

Check up on Elijah the prophet, even Jeremiah, see if their brethren didn't want to bust their brains for telling it right, like it is, yeah – these are my roots I suppose. Am I looking for them? Well, I don't know. I ain't looking for them in synagogues with six pointed Egyptian stars shining down from every window, I can tell you that much!!

Bob Dylan, 1983.

If I catch who spiked me drink, I'll break off both their arms and beat 'em to death.

Keith Moon, after collapsing on a Dallas stage, 1974.

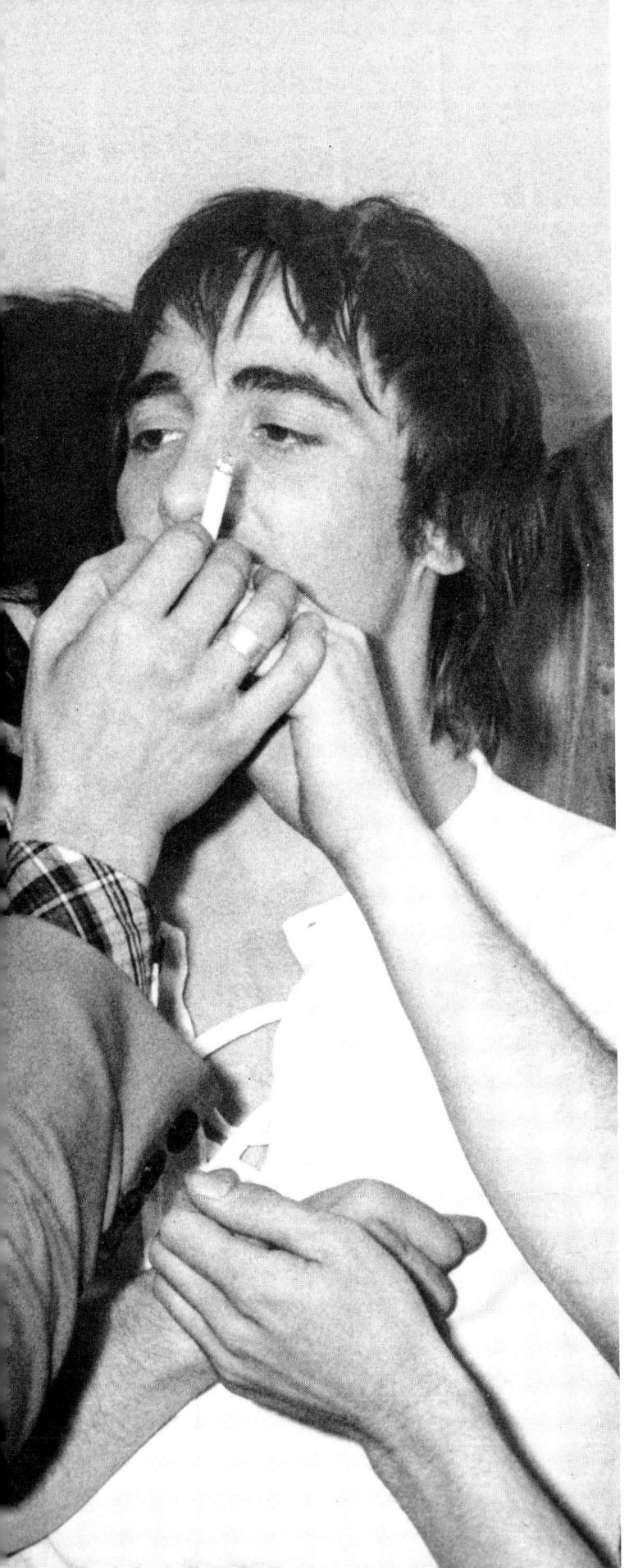

THERE WAS NO BAR. The mind recoils at the depth of insensitivity it must take to organise a Pogues concert at which everyone is compelled to stay sober.

Dave Jennings, journalist, 1988.

You know when you get a small combo – perhaps organ, bass and drums – playing in the corner of the lounge bar of your local, about half an hour before closing time, there'll invariably be a drunken, toothless idiot who staggers up to the mike and insists on mouthing 'Strangers In The Night' or 'My Way'. Inside his head he's Sinatra or Matt Monroe or the like, while outside his body limits, folk are sniggering in their beer or throwing up in the plastic tulips. Now you can enjoy this experience in the privacy of your own home.

Cliff White, journalist, reviewing Acker Bilk's 'Dancing In The Dark', 1977.

Was that the song? I thought it was the introduction!

Jet Black, The Stranglers, reviewing 'Cranked Up Really High' by Slaughter And The Dogs, 1977.

Dead, actually.

Lynden Barber, journalist, in his famed two-word review of Dead Or Alive's 'What I Want' single, 1984.

It's really hip to have a film star's name in your record now, isn't it? We must try it . . . 'Sylvester Stallone's Masturbating'...

Pete Burns, 1984.

I watched Sean Penn in *Bad Boys* just to see what Madonna saw in him. The reasons I came up with aren't very printable I'm afraid.

Marc Almond, 1985.

You watch an old film like *On The Waterfront* and you think, 'What a fuckin' incredible guy', y'know. But if you ever met 'im, I'm sure he'd be a prat.

Pete Wylie, 1981.

I don't think anybody knows who August Darnell is these days, including himself.

Elbow Bones, 1984.

They're a shitty group. Kill Coati Mundi.

Nick Cave, The Birthday Party, reviewing Kid Creole's 'Dear Addy', 1982.

Yeah, he's got lots of charm . . . I call him rat poison in spats.

Cristina, on August Darnell, 1983.

It's just that James Cagney 'I'm so short I can't get any attention' problem.

Adrienna Kaegi, The Coconuts, on Coati Mundi, 1983.

It's difficult to tell if a guy is hip, or he wears dark glasses because his eyesight's bad.

Stevie Winwood, 1966.

I'm not trying to be Alexis Colby or anything but, if something is taken out of my control, I'll bury it. No-one is getting a foot on my gravy train.

Pete Burns, 1987.

Ronnie Bond, Trogg : We used to have arguments like that all the time in rehearsal, but we usually had them sorted out by the time we got in the studio. The funny thing was, the song we were meant to be recording was called 'Tranquility'.

Reg Presley, Trogg : No it wasn't – I hadn't even written the song.

Ronnie Bond : It was. I remember there was some trouble with the chords.

Reg Presley : It bloody well was not, you fucking pranny.

1984.

I think Bryan Ferry is sadly lacking in style. I saw him on TV, he came on in a tuxedo, and then took it off. I thought, this is the sort of man who walks into the restaurant and rolls his sleeves up.

Martin Fry, ABC, 1983.

I was cramping Eno's style. Two non-musicians in a band is one too many.

Bryan Ferry, on Roxy Music's keyboard player, 1973.

As soon as he was in the studio, he was up the bar ordering doubles.

John, King Kurt, on producer Dave Edmunds, 1984.

I really believe I *should* slag Blancmange off, because they have no redeeming features.

Julian Cope, 1983.

When people like Green and Mark E. Smith criticise me so obsessively, to me it's like an underhand admiration, that they should dedicate so many hours in the day to actually thinking about me. Because I certainly don't think about them.

Morrissey, 1984.

You know we did *The Tube* right? The best thing that happened to us was . . . you saw that kid who came on with The Smiths? Yeah well, he was in the hospitality room, which of course The Smiths never went in, and the kid was eyeing us up in our strange garments. He put Cobalt's jacket and shades on and then he said to Cobalt, 'I wish I was in your group instead of The Smiths!' . . . That was really brilliant.

Zodiac Mindwarp, 1986.

Sigue Sigue who? I've never heard of them.

Michael Rutherford, Genesis, 1986.

We've always maintained that if we *wanted* to play Genesis-type stuff, we could.

The Smiths . . . drab music for drab people.

Tony James, 1985.

I had always listened to Genesis and liked them an awful lot, though I can only listen to them once a year now.

Ian Astbury, The Cult, 1985.

Au Contraire to popular belief, there is no *NME* party line on anything – never has been and never will be. It just happens that we all sincerely loathe Genesis.

Paul Du Noyer, journalist, 1983.

Susan and Norman, you dreary couple with the Ford Cortina and your names on the windscreen. There's actually a Susan and Norman out there right now, driving around in a blue Ford Cortina, feeling well proud of themselves for being so utterly dull.

Johnny Rotten, 1986.

I've been speaking to, like, 20-year-old fanzine writers, and they'll be asking me what the 'White Riot' tour was like, or what it was like to see The Buzzcocks, or whether I ever saw The Buzzcocks with Howard Devoto. I mean, COME ON. It would be like me in 1977 going up to people saying, '*Hey*, did you see The Grateful Dead?' It's over. All that was 10 years ago. Surely now it's time to put your best foot forward.

Edwyn Collins, 1986.

The whole thing about '76 and '77 has been totally romanticised. There were only a couple of other bands who were worth anything, and they turned out to be real wankers in the end.

Paul Weller, on his Jam days, 1985.

I think The Jam are one of the worst groups in the world.

Jim Reid, The Jesus And Mary Chain, 1985.

I don't really give a fuck any more about what anyone thinks of me.

Paul Weller, 1985.

I have a toilet mentality – I don't give a shit what people know about me.

Linda Thompson, 1985.

Some nights he'd have us in tears of laughter but, after about five months on the road, it would start to feel like you were on tour with Tommy Cooper.

Chris Difford, Squeeze, on Jools Holland, 1981.

When you've got nine billion subjects in the world, why confine what you talk about to people from a couple of different countries and the mother of the person you've married?

Alexei Sayle, 1984.

Herpes is forever.

Janie Jones, 1984.

If these are her greatest musical hits, then only one little piece of advice should be given. Keep your daughter *on* the stage Mrs Willcox.

Barry McIlheney, journalist, reviewing 'Toyah! Toyah! Toyah! — All The Hits,' 1984.

. . . Presumably you pay this idiot to write reviews, so why not get him to do it in English?

Andy, Guildford, letter to the Melody Maker, 1983.

So they said to me, 'Take off your hat' — and I said, 'That's my hair!' . . . Huh.

Toyah, 1981.

Bugger off, you stupid bunch of hacks!

Glitterbest, 1978.

They seem to think that if you sing about something, then some kid is automatically going to go out and copy it. If that was the case, every teenager in America would have a gun and go

round shooting people after watching *Miami Vice*. It's insane. And anyway, how many people you know can afford a guillotine?!

Alice Cooper, on *his* critics, 1986.

Why do you print so many f***ing asterisks in your f***ing excellent paper? The effect of these stars is not obliterative, nay, it gives undue prescience and importance to often trivial and flippant uses of expletives. What is this? Are you censored? Or are you just trying to make teenagers giggle?

Richard Baker, letter to the Melody Maker, 1988.

Mary Whitehouse has to go and see something nine times before she makes up her mind whether it's pornographic or not. There's something in that.

Roger Daltrey, 1975.

It did seem impossible for her to go on . . . she would have needed a portable toilet on stage after every number.

Marty Balin, Jefferson Starship, on Grace Slick's departure from the group, 1978.

The Doctors Of Madness were like John Kennedy, in that they were never more popular than the day after they died.

Richard Strange, 1982.

Well, old John Barton's back from his dead-end job, sub-editing the 'Exit' brochure . . .

Malc The Knife, Marlow, letter to the *Melody Maker*, 1983.

Dead.

James King, on Jim Reeves, 1986.

I'm really chained to those iron bridges, I'm really chained to the pier. I'm persistently on some disused clearing in Wigan. I shall be buried there, I'm sure, and shall be glad to go at that point. I mean I certainly don't want to be buried at Rough Trade!!

Morrissey, 1984.

The press made it into a big thing – 'rock star's body burned in ritual' – it wasn't a ritual, it was a deal, something I'd promised him. Everybody I knew understood that. I saw Keith Richards and he hugged me and said 'Nice one Phil, you took care of Gram' – I nearly said 'You're next!' The shape he was in you shouldn't smoke around him, he might go up.

Phil Kaufman, on the burning of Gram Parsons' body, 1981.

You look like a million dollars today . . . All green and wrinkled.

Chris Foreman, to Paolo Hewitt, journalist, 1984.

The Falklands . . . basically, it was old people sending young people down.

Ian Hunter, 1983.

Anybody naïve enough to think they're going into the army to learn a trade deserves to get their head blown off.

Fad Gadget, 1982.

I'm still waiting for Nick Kent to appear on Arthur C. Clarke's programme. Why this man thinks he's a journalist is a mystery to me.

Lew Grant, letter to the *NME*, 1980.

It's not that we're too clever, it's just that everybody else is too thick.

Terry Chambers, XTC, 1982.

I have never even *heard* of Einsturzende Neubauten.

Nena, 1984.

I don't put people down for taking my style and finding something of their own, but I don't think Tom Robinson has found anything original yet. He's only saying things that I said on 'Preservation' – I don't think there's anything original there. *I* am an original.

Ray Davies, The Kinks, 1978.

We only got one glass thrown at us in those two years, and it's typical of us that it wasn't a pint glass, but a little liquor glass. Even the people who didn't like us threw wimpy glasses!

Grant McLennan, The Go-Betweens, on the group's early days, 1982.

That was before Jobson started dressing like Val Doonican.

Boy George remembers The Skids, 1983.

I've never been his lover, not once. I don't fancy him in the slightest.

Marilyn, on Boy George, 1984.

Ray Davies has always been an old man. He writes like an old man who is forever looking back on his life.

Pete Townshend, 1975.

I don't say they've deliberately copied Bono and Co – but there are times when, like Scott of the Antarctic, you've just got to accept that Amundsen has got there before you, and go off and try something else.

Paul Du Noyer, journalist, on Silent Running, 1983.

I kinda skip over interviews and go straight to the quotes if I'm interested in the person. I'm always looking for the quotation marks. I'm quite interested to see what groups have to say for themselves. I remember being put off by people like Paul Morley in the late seventies, all that now-pop wow-pop yow-pop kind of thing. Could never be bothered with all that . . .

Roddy Frame, Aztec Camera, 1988.

We're giving you the opportunity to write very well. If you don't write very well, we won't be doing another interview with *Record Mirror*.

Freya Miller, Shakin' Stevens' manager, 1981.

If someone says to me, 'Watch that person, they're in a position to really slag you' – then I just go up and say, 'You cunt, I hate you' . . . I really don't need all that.

Johnny Rotten, 1977.

My favourite bitch? . . . Annie Walker in *Coronation Street*. She has some of the best, most acid lines. Like Elsie Tanner said to her, 'Do you like my dress?' – and she turned to Elsie and said, 'My dear, I've *always* liked your dress,' ha-ha!

Marc Almond, 1982.

Have you come to stitch us up then?

Mark O'Toole, Frankie Goes To Hollywood, greeting Ted Mico, journalist, 1986.

No matter what you write, they sub it. Even if you do a dissertation on Dostoevsky, they'd still make it sound like John Blake.

Muriel Grey, media personality, on publishers, 1987.

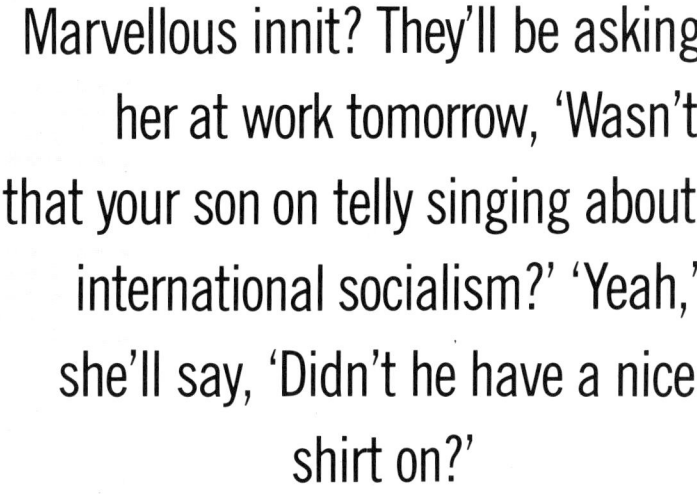

Marvellous innit? They'll be asking her at work tomorrow, 'Wasn't that your son on telly singing about international socialism?' 'Yeah,' she'll say, 'Didn't he have a nice shirt on?'

Billy Bragg, on his mum's response to his appearance on *Top Of The Pops*, **1985.**

I can't stand anyone else having the last word.

Pete Burns, Dead Or Alive, 1984.